JUST THE THREE WEEKS IN PROVENCE

JUST THE THREE WEEKS
IN PROVENCE

Travels with the Scotland Squad and
the Tartan Army in World Cup '98

Tom Shields and Ken Gallacher

MAINSTREAM
PUBLISHING

EDINBURGH AND LONDON

First published in Great Britain in 1998 by
MAINSTREAM PUBLISHING COMPANY (EDINBURGH) LTD
7 Albany Street
Edinburgh EH1 3UG

ISBN 1 84018 130 3

A catalogue record for this book is available from the British Library

Typeset in Sabon
Printed and bound in Great Britain by Butler & Tanner Ltd

Contents

PART I

THE TEAM

Ken Gallacher

This is for my grandson Scott Mackie who enlisted in the Foreign Legion of the Tartan Army in St-Etienne and learned at first hand the heartbreak which anyone following Scotland is forced to suffer.

Prologue

It seems inconceivable now to the members of the Tartan Army, to the Scotland international players and even to the game's administrators, that the love affair which the nation has enjoyed for the last quarter of a century with the World Cup, was a late-blooming event.

So slow, indeed, was the realisation that the World Cup would become the major football extravaganza that it is today, that back in 1950 Scotland declined to take part in the finals which were held in Brazil.

The country was invited along with England as FIFA sought to re-establish itself and its competition in the aftermath of the Second World War. But the powers that be – those who ran the Scottish Football Association back then – took the stance that Scotland would only travel to South America if they won the British International Championship, a tournament they still viewed as the major international event in world football. The British title was to be decided – as it almost always was – with the annual clash between Scotland and England. The Scots had enjoyed a good season with a massive 8–2 win in Belfast against Northern Ireland with goals from Henry Morris who scored a hat-trick but who was never capped again; two more from Willie Waddell; while Billy Steel, Lawrie Reilly and Jimmy Mason also scored. The national side continued with a 2–0 win over Wales at Hampden and, with England having to come to Glasgow, it seemed that Scotland were favourites to win back-to-back British titles.

When England duly arrived in Glasgow in April, however, for the match which would decide whether or not the Scots would play in the World Cup for the first time, things went against the home country. Roy Bentley scored for England, the Hearts striker

Willie Bauld hit the bar and the Scots stayed at home, oblivious to what was happening on the other side of the Atlantic. In retrospect, perhaps, Bauld's miss was a blessing in disguise, as England found themselves humbled by the United States of America in a game which has never been forgotten. And which never will. That 1–0 defeat in Belo Horizonte probably remains the worst humiliation England have ever suffered.

The tournament was won by Uruguay who defeated the host nation Brazil in the final in Rio but, that England shock apart, the competition passed virtually unnoticed in Scotland. It was an event taking place far away from our own shores and involving players we scarcely knew anything about. The Scottish Football Association were scarcely criticised for their decision to snub the FIFA invitation. Quite simply, in Scotland the whole affair just didn't count for all that much.

Four years later attitudes had not altered a great deal, though, with the tournament being played in Switzerland, the men from Glasgow's Carlton Place (where the SFA headquarters were then located) did accept the offer from FIFA asking Scotland to take part. But they did so in a half-hearted and haphazard way, as if still unconvinced about the value of the FIFA event.

For example, Rangers, who had such international players as George Young, Sammy Cox and Willie Waddell in their team, went off on a close-season tour of Canada and the United States and their Scotland players went with them. No one at the SFA made any formal objections to the fact that the Ibrox club looked on a summer jaunt across the Atlantic as being more important than the World Cup finals. The tournament had still not impinged sufficiently on the consciousness of the nation to be seen as something truly important in the development of football.

Tommy Docherty looks back on Scotland's debut as one of the biggest farces he encountered in his long career in the game. He recalls: 'I think we only took around 14 players with us to the finals. The Rangers lads didn't go because they were off on tour to the States. People find it hard to believe nowadays, but it's true. We hadn't a clue as to what it was all about. We had more officials in the travelling party than we had players.

'Then when we actually went out on to the field to play the games things became even more farcical. Someone in authority, someone in the SFA, had decided that it was going to be cold in Switzerland in the summer. After all, you were always seeing

pictures of snow-capped mountains and the like, and so we were
kitted out for a Hampden game in December. We had these heavy
woollen jerseys and the socks were the same and the temperature
was up in the seventies and it was a nightmare. It wasn't quite as
bad against Austria in the first game when we lost 1–0, but then
we came up against the holders Uruguay in Basle and it was really
hot. We looked along at their team and they were all lined up
before the match in lightweight gear while we were sweating
before the game started. Their national anthem went on forever
and I thought at one stage I was going to pass out in the heat while
this music went on and on and on . . .

'Eventually we lost 7–0, the worst defeat Scotland had ever
suffered, and it was a game we all wanted to forget. The South
Americans were playing a different game from us. I think a lot of
the players knew then that football was developing around the
world and leaving us behind.'

The result shocked the country. No one could quite grasp what
had happened. The old belief that Scotland had given the game to
the world and should remain its acknowledged master took a
hammering as the public started to wake up to the fact that most
of the world was now playing the game, and more and more
countries were playing it better than the Scots were.

For the finals in 1958, Scotland had to qualify as the
tournament's importance grew and there was a slowly growing
awareness that the World Cup was a competition of some
importance. I can remember travelling through from Dundee to
see a hat-trick from Jackie Mudie and another goal from the
Charlton full-back, South African-born John Hewie, give Scotland
a famous victory over Spain. I was there at Hampden again six
months later when the Scots won 3–2 against Switzerland. While
there was a revenge win for Spain in Madrid, the Scots had
defeated the Swiss earlier in Basle and that 2–1 win – with goals
from Mudie and Bobby Collins – was enough to carry them into
the finals in Sweden, there on merit for the first time, instead of
being asked along to make up the numbers.

Those finals in 1958 brought the breakthrough in recognition
which had been missing in Scotland on the two previous occasions
the team had played in the finals. This was, after all, the year of
Pele and of Garrincha, too. And of Vava and of Nilton Santos.

On flickering black and white television screens of maybe 12 or
14 inches in size, we marvelled at the dazzling new concept of the

game which was presented to the world and dared to wonder if Scotland would ever be able to reach these heights. I suppose now the supporters still wonder, though now they do so with despair rather than with the hope which was evident 40 years ago.

The performances Scotland gave in the tournament did nothing to suggest that any lessons had been learned after the débâcle against Uruguay in Basle. This time the team opened with a creditable draw against Yugoslavia when Hearts forward Jimmy Murray scored, but they slumped to defeat against Paraguay where two goals from Jackie Mudie and Bobby Collins were not enough to stave off a 3–2 loss. In the last group game against France in Orebro, Sammy Baird got Scotland's goal as they went down 2–1 and, inevitably, left for home early.

When the next competition came round, the finals were staged in Chile and Scotland missed out on the opportunity to go to South America once again. Yet, a powerful case can be made for the quality of the team which failed to get past the qualifying stages that time. They succumbed to Czechoslovakia in a play-off game in Brussels after finishing level with them in a three-team section which had also included the Republic of Ireland. Ian St John scored twice in the Belgian capital but it was not enough to stop the Czechs who marched on towards Chile; there they reached the final of the tournament only to lose to the Brazilians in Santiago. Denis Law, Pat Crerand, Jim Baxter, Ian St John and Billy McNeill were some of the Scotland stars.

When you examine how close they pushed the Czechs and remember their victory over that very fine side from Eastern Europe at Hampden in the home game, then you realise that this might have been the best Scottish team who failed to qualify. Given how well the Czechs did, the Scots might even have made a mark on the finals if they had been able to get to Chile that summer.

Instead, the stars went on their summer holidays and pondered on how the Fates had conspired to place them in the group alongside the country which proved itself the best in Europe at that time. That generation of players – Law apart – was destined to miss out on any other World Cup finals, because after Sweden and the 1958 finals it was to be 16 long years before the country qualified again.

There always seemed to be banana skins along the way, traps which were sprung whenever Scotland walked on to the world stage seeking the glory which was forever out of reach. When the qualifying matches for 1966 were drawn, the Scots found themselves bracketed with Italy – already perennial qualifiers for what was now becoming the world's greatest sporting occasion. This time the team were being willed to victory as the fans knew the finals were being played across the border in England. The thought of all the glamour and all the glitz being staged just a few hundred miles away was going to be too much to bear if Scotland could not be there to join football's élite. Again, though, it was not to be. Again, the Scottish team failed to get past the group stages; and this time they could not point to the success in the finals of the country which knocked them out and take some consolation from that. Italy did not do a Czechoslovakia. Uncharacteristically, they flopped.

When Italy lost to North Korea in Middlesbrough, effigies of the team were burned in Rome and when they returned from England the players and their manager, Dr Edmondo Fabbri, were pelted with rotten fruit. They slunk home in disgrace and yet, the Italians had been good enough to defeat Scotland in Naples by a 3–0 margin, though they had lost 1–0 at Hampden when John Greig scored.

Naples in 1966 was a disaster. The team had already slipped up against Poland at Hampden, but that last qualifying match in Italy brought nothing but heartbreak for the Scottish team. Beforehand the temporary team manager, Celtic's Jock Stein, had been hit with one crisis after another. Neither of the nation's two biggest stars, Denis Law and Jim Baxter, were available for selection for the game – although Baxter somehow played for his club Sunderland in a match 24 hours before the Naples clash. There was a goalkeeping worry too, after Bobby Ferguson, the young Kilmarnock keeper, lost six goals against Real Madrid in a European tie just a week before the Italy game. His confidence was shredded and Stein dashed south the weekend before the World Cup decider to see Burnley's veteran Adam Blacklaw. Blacklaw travelled north by sleeper to join the squad before flying out and playing in the game. On the eve of the match, Rangers's winger Willie Henderson was injured in training and forced to call off and Scotland went out with a makeshift team as the World Cup curse struck them with a vengeance. It is difficult to believe now that preparations could be so sketchy, but the national team were still at the mercy of the clubs and the release of players could not be demanded if the men in question were playing outside Scotland. That was just something that Scotland had to live with.

Italy had transferred the game to Naples because they reckoned that the fans there would intimidate the Scots. It was always the venue of choice when they felt that victory was essential and that every weapon at their disposal had to be used. In the event they needed a little help from outside agencies as the Scotland team crashed to a three-goal defeat in a match which had been lost before kick-off as Stein's plans had been wrecked and wrecked again by call-offs, lapses in form and late injuries. It was just another black afternoon in the country's World Cup history, one that seems to be forever repeated at some stage of the tournament.

The next time round, with the finals set to be staged in Mexico in 1970, the Scots recognised immediately that they would have the greatest difficulty in qualifying when they were drawn in the same group as West Germany, never-failing contestants in the final stages and winners in 1954 in Switzerland, as well as unfortunate runners-up to England in the Wembley final which climaxed the previous tournament.

Scotland began the tournament well. They defeated Austria at Hampden with goals from Denis Law and Billy Bremner and then won 5–0 in Nicosia against Cyprus when Alan Gilzean and Colin Stein each collected two goals, the other coming from Bobby Murdoch. It was Murdoch, again, in the home match against the Germans who scored, but that was only enough to give the team a draw after a Franz Beckenbauer free-kick had set up his Bayern team-mate, Gerd Muller, for the German goal.

No matter that Scotland were able to hammer eight goals past the Cypriots in the home game, the return against Germany loomed.

The goals at Hampden came from Colin Stein (4), Eddie Gray, Billy McNeill, Willie Henderson and Tommy Gemmell and while the Scots had managed a total of 13 goals against the poor relations of the group, Germany scraped through against them away from home – thanks to a goal from Muller in injury time. The Scottish players and manager Bobby Brown knew that a draw in West Germany could yet be enough to take the country to the finals and there was an air of confidence when the side went to Hamburg for the return. The Germans had always insisted that they found Scots difficult opposition and there was a feeling in the travelling party that this was to be the opportunity to upset the group favourites.

It didn't happen. The Scots were close, desperately close, but the cards had been stacked against them before the game. The wily German coach Helmut Schoen somehow prevailed upon Bobby Brown to allow the veteran German striker Uwe Seeler to walk on to the field on his own in front of his Hamburg fans. While that happened, while the roars of acclaim swept down from the Volksparkstadion terracings, the Scotland team stood around at one end of the pitch like extras in a movie extravaganza without even any balls to be used for shooting in. This memorable moment was what Schoen had counted on, and it went as planned with the huge crowd getting behind their team and lifting them even after a Jimmy Johnstone goal gave Scotland an early lead. Alan Gilzean also scored that night, but the Scots went down 3–2 and when the Celtic full-back Tommy Gemmell was ordered off in the second half, the dream of reaching Mexico died. In Vienna, just a couple of weeks later, Scotland lost their last group game against Austria 2–0 but, by then, the result was meaningless.

West Germany went to Mexico where Beckenbauer, Muller *et al* were to take third place behind Brazil and Italy, and give warning that they were prepared for the finals which they would host in 1974 and which, for the first time in 16 long years, would have Scotland among the 16 teams taking part.

Before departing for Manchester United as their manager, Tommy Docherty had a couple of exciting years in charge of the Scottish team and it was the irrepressible Doc who set Scotland off on the road to these finals with two victories before he took his leave for Old Trafford. Scotland were drawn in a three-country group with Czechoslovakia and Denmark. The Danes were not yet the power in world football that they have become today, but Docherty reckoned that they could still hold the key to the group, so he decided that in the opening match in Copenhagen the Scotland side had to be an attacking one, his theory being that to win away from home against the Danes could prove crucial. It did and the 4–1 victory with goals from Jimmy Bone, Lou Macari, Joe Harper and Willie Morgan set the target for the Czechs – especially as in the Hampden return a month later Scotland won again. This time the margin was 2–0 and the goals were scored by Kenny Dalglish and Peter Lorimer. When Czechoslovakia could only draw in

Copenhagen, Scotland were left knowing that a win at home against the team from Eastern Europe would guarantee qualification. By now Willie Ormond had been appointed to take over from Docherty and he knew that the one win was essential. He picked a team that night to give the nation the qualification which had seemed to have been out of reach, bringing back the veteran Denis Law and thrusting left-winger Tommy Hutchison into the side for his first cap.

Ormond's team choice was inspirational and his tactics were as successful as those of Docherty had been when the qualifying group had kicked off 11 months earlier. Although the Scots went a goal down, they came back to equalise through the late Jim Holton before half-time and then substitute Joe Jordan scored the winner against a Czech team who would be European champions two years later. The huge Hampden crowd saluted the first Scottish team to reach the finals since Sweden in 1958 as they made their lap of honour.

By now, the tournament's importance was recognised and when the draw for the finals was made in Frankfurt and Scotland were grouped along with the world champions, Brazil, as well as Yugoslavia and Zaire the nation began to prepare itself for the first major Tartan Army invasion of foreign soil.

Of course, those of us who had been following Scotland in previous campaigns should have known that things had progressed too smoothly in this particular qualification programme. That, though, was soon to be altered and in one of the more farcical occurrences which has ever struck the international side. During the Home International Championships – indeed just prior to the game against England at Hampden – there was the now notorious incident of Jimmy Johnstone and the rowing boat. The Scots had lost to Northern Ireland in their second game – earlier they had beaten Wales 2–0 – and after a night out in a local pub in Largs, where the team had its headquarters, some of the players finished up literally messing about in boats. The end result was that the little Celtic winger was set adrift by his team-mates and he floated out into the Firth of Clyde with just one oar.

The coastguards were called out as he drifted towards the horizon waving the single oar aloft and singing his heart out, blissfully unaware of any danger.

In later years the team manager Willie Ormond would see the

funny side of things and would recall: 'I heard the commotion around the hotel and down on the front and when I looked out of my bedroom window all I could see was this boat drifting away from the shore and I could hear wee Jimmy's voice as he sang and waved the oar about in the air. I couldn't believe it at first, and then when I went downstairs I found that the alarm had been raised and a rescue operation was under way. I was angry at the time and he knew that, but I played him against England on the Saturday and he was great that day and we won 2–0.'

That should have been the happy ending to the story but, given the predisposition to self-destruction which lurks within so many Scottish footballers, there was more grief to come. And from the same source at that!

The World Cup show – Scotland, remember were the sole British team to qualify – rolled onwards to Belgium and to Norway where Ormond had arranged warm-up games before moving into their training camp just outside Frankfurt. In Oslo, Jimmy Johnstone and the team captain, Leeds United's Billy Bremner, became involved in another drinking session in the team hotel. They were ordered to their rooms by a furious Ormond, but squad members still tell hilarious stories of the pair deciding that they were going back home before the expected axe fell from the SFA officials, some of whom had witnessed their high-jinks. They insisted they were leaving – and leaving that very night.

They attempted to pack their suitcases and dragged them along the hotel corridors with shirt-sleeves hanging out of the luggage and not so much as an air ticket between them. Eventually some of the other players persuaded them to stay on and one of those who did so, Davie Hay, says: 'If it had not been so potentially serious for the two of them it was one of the funniest sights you would ever have seen at any team hotel. There they were, the two of them, absolutely determined to leave and they didn't know when there were flights out of Oslo nor did they have tickets. And their cases were only half-packed with ties and socks hanging out and I spoke to them and they listened and wee Billy suddenly seemed to realise how serious the whole thing had become and the pair of them went back to their rooms. The whole thing had started because on the flight up from Brussels the aircrew had handed round champagne for the lads because we were the only British team going to West Germany. That's when things got a wee bit out of hand, but it was blown up out of all proportion as far as Jimmy and Billy were concerned and I think that Willie Ormond knew that. When the SFA met the next day the manager went to bat for the players and they were not sent home. For a spell, though, all of us thought that was what was going to happen.

'Anyway, Willie knew that he was going to need the players and Billy, as the captain and the on-field organiser, was really important, and this was happening well in advance of the finals. It was not going to affect their performances. If they had been sent home it would have disrupted the squad and done far more damage than the incident did.

'We all believed at the time that the manager was right.'

The performances by Bremner in Dortmund and Frankfurt at the three games certainly justified Ormond's stance against the punishment the Association had wanted to mete out to the players. But there was always the nagging feeling that Johnstone was left out of the games because of his indiscretions.

Although, as remains the case to this day, Scotland were unable to reach the second stage of the finals, they returned to Glasgow with their heads high after remaining unbeaten and going out on goal-difference only.

The game against Brazil remains etched in the memory almost quarter of a century later. In Frankfurt's Waldstadion the Scots were being torn apart in the opening 15 minutes of the game as Brazil swept into attack after attack, then Bremner made some adjustments to the formation and also set himself up for his personal *mano a mano* with Roberto Rivelino which ended at the final whistle with those two combative and skilled midfielders saluting each other in the centre-circle and swapping jerseys in a gesture of mutual respect. Of course, Bremner just failed to score at the post with a chance and so Scotland could only draw 0–0 and then finish with another draw, this time 2–2 with the Slavs, and that was not enough. Home they went, but hundreds of fans waited to welcome them at Glasgow Airport and I can still recall Bremner anxiously coming down the aisle of the plane as it prepared to land asking if anyone knew ALL the words of 'Amazing Grace', which was the 'Flower of Scotland' of its time. He wanted to have the players sing that as they disembarked because I think he realised – indeed I think they all realised – that they had taken part in something very special. And they had, because that was just the beginning . . .

That was when the love affair with the World Cup began. It started in West Germany, it had its roots there when the Scots beat Zaire to record their first-ever win at the finals and there, especially, when they matched the boys from Brazil in one of the national side's finest-ever performances.

The players had given the supporters memories to cherish and given themselves a reputation on the world stage which had not been there before. After an absence of 16 years, Scotland had returned to centre stage in world football and had been able to return home unbeaten and unbowed and with the ambition to return to the finals as often as possible in the future.

Four years further on they did return – but on this occasion the expedition was as ill-fated as any the international team had ever undertaken.

Argentina was the venue and even now the name of the country brings back memories best forgotten. And yet, the team had qualified with distinction, again from a three-country group and again from a group which contained Czechoslovakia – who had now been crowned European champions after defeating the World Cup holders West Germany on penalties in the final in Belgrade. The other country in the section was, of course, Wales.

By now there had been another change in manager with Willie Ormond returning to club football with Hearts and Ally MacLeod leaving Aberdeen to take on the job of handling the national side. This time, in contrast to the previous competition, Scotland kicked-off with a defeat. They went to Prague to open their challenge just months after the Czechs' European triumph, and lost 2–0 there. It was scarcely a surprise, but it was a setback from which Scotland had to recover, and recover quickly.

The following month saw an unconvincing win over Wales at Hampden that did little to raise the hopes for the supporters. It took an own goal from Alun Evans to give Scotland the points. It was to be almost a year before the team were back in action and by then there was a more settled look about the formation; when they met the Czechs in the return game in Glasgow there was more purpose about their game too. In what was one of their best qualifying performances, they stormed to a 3–1 win with goals from Joe Jordan, Asa Hartford and Kenny Dalglish. It was a performance, and a result, which had all of Europe sitting up and paying attention. The German coach Helmut Schoen used a video of that game to stress to his own players the value of the pressing game which Scotland displayed to perfection on that September night when qualification was back within their grasp.

Again it was down to one game and to one victory with the opponents, Wales, giving up home advantage and moving the game to Anfield to cash in on the expected invasion from north of the border. The Liverpool full-back Joey Jones told his team-mate Kenny Dalglish that the Welsh fans would take over the Kop. Never has anyone been so wrong. So totally and utterly wrong. The atmosphere was electric and it may have been there that the Tartan Army – the descendant of those thousands of men in tartan tammies and scarves who made the bi-annual jaunt to Wembley for the game against England – emerged as an off-field ally for the Scots.

There had been signs of its birth in West Germany, but in Liverpool that day it was in full flower with the Scotland presence being overwhelming. Walking up to the stadium I remember Jock Stein waving his arm at the sea of tartan and saying: 'Look! Just look at these people. There is no way that we can lose this game tonight, not with that backing behind the team. You can't even think of defeat. It won't happen.'

Stein was right and those who were there can still see Joey Jones's face fall as he stepped out on to the field, looked towards the Kop and saw that the Scots had taken residence there just as they had in every corner of the ground.

There was some luck on Scotland's side that night when their own 'hand of God' incident occurred when the referee decided that a Welsh defender had handled when he rose to challenge Joe Jordan in the penalty box. The French official pointed to the spot, Don Masson duly scored and then, to make certain, Kenny Dalglish helped himself to a second on his home turf and the hysteria which was to be Scotland's downfall in South America was unleashed across the land.

I now find it hard to look back on those finals in Argentina without a sense of sadness, without a feeling of regret and even of embarrassment. Could the press have shown more restraint when Ally MacLeod promised the country that the team would return with a medal? Could the football writers then – and I was one of them – have ignored the braggadocio of the team manager? Perhaps we might have, but, in the mood of the time, we would have been looked upon as traitors to the country's cause. Some of us did try to remain sensible, we did try to point out that qualification for the second stage would be enough of a target (something we were still repeating last summer in France) and talk of medals was over the top. But the people had found their Messiah and Ally MacLeod played the role to the full, until that first defeat.

In the end the fall was dreadful to behold. In the days which followed the defeat from Peru – a team the manager had failed to watch beforehand, dismissing them as a side with too many over-the-hill stars, one of whom was Cubillas who starred in the game in Cordoba – MacLeod appeared to lose his grip. There was dissension in the camp and bitter disappointment among the travelling support who had believed in all the propaganda. When the Scots slumped to a draw against Iran, MacLeod was a man in torment. All of us are still haunted by the haggard, despairing look on his face during that second match when all the dreams he had spun drifted away from him. I doubt that he has ever recovered from the trauma of these few days in Cordoba when everything just fell apart.

None of us who were there have ever been able to escape from the memories when every morning brought a fresh rumour, every day a fresh denial and there were times when some of us believed we had stumbled on to the set of a disaster movie. Almost every single allegation made against the players was subsequently proved wrong while others contained only scraps of truth. In the end, poor Willie Johnston became the scapegoat for all the ills which beset the expedition when he failed a drugs test after the opening game.

Only two journalists spoke to Johnston the day the news broke and I was one of them. The player was a shattered man, still unable to grasp the full implications of the scandal he had become embroiled in. He had taken a couple of Reactivan tablets before the game, he was quite open about that, and he had done so because he had been using the same tablets with his club.

At West Bromwich Albion he had taken them over a period of months believing they helped his performance while being totally unaware that they contained a minute amount of a drug called fencamfemeine which was on a list of banned substances which had been compiled by FIFA. Johnston, in common with most people, had not read the small print on the medicine bottle and because he had been using the tablets at his club he remained ignorant that he was using a banned substance.

Ignorance, of course, is no defence and the Scottish Football Association rightly pointed out that the team doctor had lectured the players on such dangers and had also asked them to tell him if they were taking any kind of medicine which could land them in trouble.

Within hours of Johnston being carpeted by the Association he was sent to Buenos Aires and placed on a flight back to London where his club manager, Ron Atkinson, met him. No one from the Scottish party accompanied him on that long, lonely journey home. The authorities simply washed their hands of him and I did not think that right at the time and over the years my feelings have not altered. Johnston made a mistake and for that he was pilloried. To have him become the equivalent of a non-person overnight was shameful and the players who were left in Alta Gracia were far from happy at the way their team-mate had been treated.

In any case, Johnston's behaviour did not affect the team's performance because they had lost the game and Scotland were, therefore, not punished further.

Other things also went wrong. The team were never comfortable in the hotel outside Cordoba which had been described to them as the Gleneagles of Argentina but which was far from that. It was adequate and no more. Then, too, there had been a row about bonuses to be paid during the finals and the then president of the SFA Willie Harkness had to meet the players to hammer home to them the details which had already been spelled out to the team manager. Somehow, Ally MacLeod had not passed on this information to the squad before they left for Argentina and this meant another unseemly row and embarrassment for Harkness and his secretary Ernie Walker who had put the bonus system together and who had believed that the players had been fully informed.

That was symptomatic of the problem which surrounded the 1978 finals and which led to the side's dismal displays in the opening games and it was ironic that, just when the fans had turned on the team, hurling missiles at the bus as it left the stadium after the Iran game in Cordoba, that the players eventually found form. Against Holland, always the favourites to win the section, Scotland came good. Kenny Dalglish scored once and Archie Gemmill scored twice and Holland were beaten 3–2, with one of Gemmill's goals among the best of the tournament. Of course, that narrow victory was not enough to allow the Scots to move forward but at least there was some consolation for the bewildered and saddened remnants of the Tartan Army to take with them on the marathon trek home.

It was only months later when MacLeod realised his position was untenable that he quit the international job and returned to club football and sanity and reason returned.

When all this happened, Jock Stein, who had quit Celtic after being insulted by a job offer made to him by the Parkhead club when Billy McNeill was appointed manager, had joined Leeds United. However, the Scottish Football Association had learned that Stein had not settled into the job and had yet to sign the long-term contract which the Elland Road club had prepared for him. The SFA made their overtures and Stein, who had been approached before and who had, remember, been in charge on a part-time basis in the mid-'60s, at last agreed to accept the post. It was a job which appeared to be ideal for him. After his years of glory with Celtic at home and in Europe, Stein was now the elder statesman of the Scottish game. He was hugely respected across the whole of Britain as well as Europe and, after the débâcle of Argentina, he was the perfect man to move into Park Gardens and rebuild faith in the team and restore dignity to the Association itself. It was a massive task and Stein was the only man who had the stature, the authority and the experience to handle it in all its various facets.

Stein had watched the hysteria build and was worried where it might lead. He knew when he was sounded out initially that a great deal of work had to be done but he knew, also, that it was important for the whole of Scottish football that the damage done to the game during the finals in Argentina had to be repaired. In essence, the offer came at the right time for Stein and for Scotland. He was unhappy at Leeds because his wife was reluctant to move south away from her family. And he knew that the Scotland job would give him the nationwide acceptance that had not been granted him in his years with Celtic.

Firstly, though, he had to put an end to the hysteria and to the over-the-top optimism which had been so much a part of MacLeod's reign. This was, though, to be a quiet revolution: one where no promises would be made, where much of the talking would be done on the park by the players. Stein recognised that success in some limited form was expected and that the World Cup in Spain in four years' time was the target he had to meet. The European Championships could be spent regrouping and the support would be tolerant of that – but when the World Cup came around again Stein and the players would be expected to deliver. It was his job to bring credibility back to the national side and not only credibility, but also a measure of dignity to the Scottish game. The SFA believed Stein was the man to do all these things for the benefit of the team and for the fans who had been so grievously let down by that Argentinian expedition.

There were a lot of pieces to be picked up, a lot of broken hearts to be mended and a new team which had to rise from the ashes of Argentina. Major surgery was required and Stein knew what had to be done. There was a resurgence on its way at club level and it arrived in time for Stein to utilise home-grown talent once again. At Aberdeen and at Dundee United, brave new worlds were being created by two of the brightest young managers in the game – Alex Ferguson and Jim McLean. These men and their clubs were to make powerful inroads on the monopoly which the Glasgow giants, Celtic and Rangers, had enjoyed for so long. The 'New Firm', as the two clubs were soon dubbed, had strong squads of players who were reaching maturity at the same time as their managers. It was no surprise, therefore, when Stein asked Jim McLean to join him.

McLean was the senior of the two New Firm men who were making such an impression on the Scottish game. Stein knew he required an assistant who knew the players and who could be trusted and McLean filled the role for several years as his players, and those from Aberdeen, began to become Scotland regulars as well.

Stein, of course, knew that to put a squad together after Argentina was not going to be easy and when he began to get the players he wanted and fit them into the international scene he was ready to face his first full World Cup adventure. (He had been in charge of several of Scotland's qualifying games on a part-time basis only back prior to the 1966 finals in England.)

The draw, though, stressed just how difficult the task would be. Sweden and Portugal posed the major threats, but also in the section were Northern Ireland and, as a wild card, Israel – there because political problems kept them out of their normal geographical area. It was to be a section fraught with danger and it was not one where Scotland could be guaranteed one of the two places which were on offer for the finals. Both the Swedes and the Portuguese had strong World Cup pedigrees, while the Irish had an exceptional squad of players which had been gathered together by their astute team manager Billy Bingham. Israel were less well known but the journey there and the conditions the Scots would face were not likely to make it easy to collect the away victory which could well be necessary for qualification. Stein knew all of that better than anyone. And, yet, somehow he guided his team to an opening victory in Stockholm against the Swedes in a game which was to prove utterly crucial in a group which was as close as you ever get for the teams involved in the qualifying rounds.

Gordon Strachan scored that night in the Swedish capital but, almost immediately, the advantage was given away when Scotland could only draw against Portugal at Hampden. Indeed, that grand old Scottish ground was not to prove the major ally it had been in previous times. While Kenny Dalglish scored the solitary goal of the match in Tel Aviv to maintain the hundred per cent record away from home, the next month brought another share of the points in Glasgow. On this occasion Northern Ireland drew 1–1, with John Wark getting the goal and allowing the team to limp forward to two more home games when, at last, the victories came. John Robertson and Davie Provan scored in the 3–0 win over Israel, while Robertson, again, and Joe Jordan struck in the second win over Sweden. Two away games were left, and on a miserable October night in Belfast Scotland survived to get a 0–0 draw against the Northern Irish which was enough to guarantee a place in the finals. Indeed, it was also enough to take the Irish through as well when Portugal slipped in their own game that night against Sweden. The Irish finished two points behind Scotland and a slender single point ahead of Sweden with the Portuguese another point behind them. Four points separated the top four teams.

So, after Scotland had been the sole British representative in West Germany and then Argentina, when the 1982 finals began in Spain they shared the stage there with England and Northern Ireland – and it was these two nations who progressed to the later stages while Scotland again wondered at the bad luck which haunted the team in this tournament. Again they were drawn with Brazil, with Russia and New Zealand making up the group.

It was there that manager Jock Stein first talked about the 'self-inflicted wounds' which cost the nation so dearly. There was no need to worry that things would be wrong off the field, not with Stein in charge, but even he could not legislate for the errors which happened during the games – particularly the last game in Malaga against the Russians. The team went into the game with hope of qualification that night, even though Stein had dropped Kenny Dalglish for the match. Before that final 90 minutes Scotland had defeated New Zealand 5–2 – though these goals from the New Zealanders, the only ones they scored in Spain, were to help cost Scotland their place at the next stage – and lost 4–1 to Brazil.

The goals in the opener had come from Dalglish, John Wark with two, John Robertson and Steve Archibald. Then in Seville it was David Narey who scored a spectacular first goal in the game with the Brazilians. Later, Graeme Souness said plaintively to me: 'I loved it when the goal went in but I soon wished we hadn't scored because all it did was get them angry!'

Stung into retaliation the Brazilian team, which included Junior and Zico and Falcao and Socrates, switched on the style and their goals came from Zico, with a stunning free-kick, Eder, Falcao and Oscar.

Everything rested on the result in the last game, and with Russia having the better goal-difference, Scotland had to win. Inevitably, it ended in a draw and the second Russian goal followed one of the most freakish incidents ever to hit a Scotland international team. Two of the most highly respected defenders in British football found themselves at the centre of the bizarre mistake.

Aberdeen's Willie Miller and Liverpool's Alan Hansen both went to clear the same ball which had been played forward towards the Scottish goal. The score was 1–1 with Joe Jordan having scored for Scotland and Chivadze getting the Russians' equaliser. Then, as the two players moved out of the penalty box and forward to meet the ball, they collided. The stunned Tartan Army could not believe what they had just witnessed and within a moment their hopes were dashed. The ball broke clear and fell perfectly for Schengeliya, who moved in on goal and struck the ball into the net. While Graeme Souness pulled a goal back before the end with a wonder-strike the World Cup was all over for the Scots yet again.

The Irish, in the meantime, beat the host nation Spain in their group and went on to play in the next phase where they drew with

Austria and lost to the brilliant French side. England, too, progressed to that stage but Germany went through from their section. But, by now, Scotland were at home trying to assess what went wrong.

Hansen told me that he had never watched videos of the incident – he didn't need to, it was forever there in his mind being replayed whenever he thought about these finals and the manner in which the Scotland side went out. Stein didn't blame the players, he stood by them, seemingly accepting that mistakes do happen even to the finest of footballers.

Stein, the greatest manager Scotland had produced, had now learned for himself the frustrations of managing the national team in the World Cup. Tragically, that was to be his first and last appearance at the finals.

The draw Scotland achieved against Wales took them on to the qualifying game against Australia on a home-and-away basis. Stein had taken the team to victories over Spain and Iceland at Hampden and Iceland in Rekyjavik but, somehow, on a night when qualification was within Scotland's grasp, Wales closed them down at Hampden and everything was down to that last match in Cardiff. At Ninian Park a Davie Cooper penalty gave Scotland the result they needed – allowing them to pip Wales by a goal to get to the play-off games – by the time these matches were played Alex Ferguson was in charge of the national side.

It was during this match that Stein had partially collapsed in the dug-out, then staggered up the tunnel and despite all efforts made to revive him he died. The players did not know until after the game and hundreds of fans stood silently for news outside the ground. When his death was announced one of them turned and said: 'We'll probably qualify for Mexico now, but I think we would rather miss out on the World Cup and have Big Jock back.'

Stein had brought in Alex Ferguson to replace Jim McLean – who had asked to stand down – and the two men worked well together. Now Fergie was asked to finish the job while still continuing as manager of Aberdeen. In November, goals from Cooper and Frank McAvennie saw Scotland defeat Australia at Hampden and two weeks later the team drew 0–0 in Melbourne to confirm their place in the Mexican finals.

Ferguson, though, soon found out the problems which can affect teams at the finals. The hotel which had been chosen was outside Mexico City where Scotland would play two of their games. The route from the city was a dismal one. Shanty towns lined the main road and the hotel itself had small rooms and few of the comforts that the modern footballer enjoyed with his club. It was not the ideal choice and Ferguson had to accept the accommodation he was given for the players. While that was a problem which had occurred in Mexico, another had struck before the team left when Kenny Dalglish, now player-manager at Liverpool, had called off when he was told he had to undergo a close-season operation. It would have been an astonishing fourth successive appearance for Dalglish at the finals, but it was not to be and the squad was seriously weakened by that loss.

There were other tensions, too, in the camp. Some months before the departure for Mexico, Graeme Souness had accepted the offer from Rangers to take over as manager at Ibrox. Like Dalglish he was to continue as a player and he was still the Scotland captain, but there were those who felt that the new Rangers manager had part of his mind on the massive job which lay ahead of him when he returned from Mexico to begin his revolution at home.

The fact that he had been involved in setting up complicated transfer deals while in Santa Fe for the specialist training, reinforced the view which was held by some observers that his priorities were elsewhere and that he should be left out of Ferguson's plans. Finally, before the last game, Ferguson did drop the highly influential Souness from the game against Uruguay. It was a mistake because the experience and the ruthless streak which Souness could use when necessary were weapons which would have been used to Scotland's advantage. It was a mistake and one which Ferguson bravely and honestly owned up to some time later at a very public appearance in Glasgow.

Scotland's section had been dubbed the 'Group of Death' when it was drawn before the finals. West Germany, Denmark and Uruguay were Scotland's opponents and it did not get much more difficult than that. When the team lost 1–0 to the Danes and Charlie Nicholas was crippled by a cruel and reckless tackle, things looked bleak for the Scots. It was a powerful Danish team with Elkjaer Larsen who scored in that first game, with Michael Laudrup, Soren Lerby and Jesper Olsen among their stars. In fact, Denmark were strong enough to beat West Germany 2–0, although they crashed out to Spain in the quarter-finals. Denmark also defeated the Uruguayans 6–1, while up in Querretaro the

Scots lost again to West Germany by 2–1. Gordon Strachan scored first but then Rudi Voeller and Klaus Allofs struck and Scotland's dreams were again placed on hold.

Despite the team making such a dismal start there was still the opportunity for qualification if they could defeat the shattered South Americans who had been humiliated by the Danes.

Certainly, Uruguay had been able to draw with West Germany in their first match, but that six-goal mauling had damaged them and Scotland felt that, perhaps, they could take advantage of the situation. They were not prepared for the utter cynicism that the Uruguayan players demonstrated. They had a player sent off in the opening minutes after Gordon Strachan – their target for the day – had been scythed to the ground. But even with the extra man, the Scotland team found themselves unable to break down the Uruguayan defence and unable to combat the incessant fouling which took place. Afterwards, Ernie Walker of the Scottish Football Association branded Uruguay 'animals', and they had sanctions imposed against them by FIFA at a meeting the following day. But they were allowed to go into the last 16, where Argentina beat them 1–0. Again, though, Scotland had returned home, back from the slums which surrounded the stadium in Neza, away from the shanty towns which were scattered around their headquarters and back to find a new manager – Alex Ferguson refused all attempts to persuade him to stay on in the job. He had his loyalties to Aberdeen and he still relished the day-to-day involvement with club football and he went back to Pittodrie before being lured to Old Trafford and Manchester United. That was the job he had always dreamed of and now it was his. Andy Roxburgh, the SFA's national coach, took over the reins of the full Scotland team to launch the country into a new era, where a high-profile coach was not considered an essential. This time the SFA, after accepting that Ferguson was not available, made the promotion from inside their own organisation, and Roxburgh was to remain at the helm for seven years.

This was not the appointment the public wanted, and when Roxburgh walked into his first press conference as the newly appointed team manager he confessed: 'I know that people will be asking "Andy who?" when they hear about this.'

It was an unfortunate remark, unprovoked by any of the questions he was asked to field, and one which was to rebound on him many times – perhaps too many for his own liking – in the years which followed. He was not the people's choice, but anyone with a knowledge of the workings of the game recognised that most of the top names which were being bandied about would not have accepted the job. The Scottish Football Association realised that and in any case they knew that Roxburgh was highly respected around the world for his coaching abilities. The burgeoning reputation was enough to throw him in at the deep end and place him in charge of a team which was in an inevitable transition period. The mainstays of the team had been Kenny Dalglish and Graeme Souness, but these two players who were known across Europe were now preparing to step aside and concentrate on their player-manager roles. Dalglish was to play just twice more in the European Championship qualifying games – against Bulgaria and Luxembourg – while Souness never played again following the finals in Mexico.

The new man was left to reconstruct the national side without the two star players – a daunting task for anyone but, still, a situation Roxburgh took on board. There were disappointments for him in the European games, but he knew that the focus was firmly on qualification for the next World Cup finals which were scheduled for Italy in 1990 and Europe was expendable.

The game in Europe, while Roxburgh would have preferred better results and even qualification, served ultimately as a means of finding his feet and finding players who would be able to help the team reach Italia '90. When the draw was made, Scotland were grouped alongside France and Yugoslavia, as well as Norway – not the force then that they have since become – and Cyprus. Roxburgh looked at that formidable line-up and realised that he would need all the luck he could get if he was to succeed in reaching what had become the Holy Grail for the Tartan Army: the World Cup finals.

As well as the dreams of the fans he knew, too, that the finals had become of paramount importance to the Association. It was a far cry now from the time in 1950 when the men who ran the game in Scotland were not interested in going to Rio. The cash on offer if the team made it to the finals was growing massively every four years and the qualifying games attracted massive crowds to Hampden. There were millions of pounds at stake now, when, in times gone by, the Association had relied on its bi-annual clash with England – now ended – for the bulk of its revenue.

It was now imperative that Scotland qualified, and continued to qualify, if the game was to continue to prosper and the Association was going to be able to finance its grass-roots coaching schemes.

Roxburgh was aware of this – he combined his team-manager duties with those of national coach after all – and when he was able to take the team to Oslo and start with a 2–1 win – thanks to goals from Paul McStay and Mo Johnston – things looked good.

However, as always, there were hiccups along the rocky road to the finals. Firstly came a 1–1 draw with the Slavs at Hampden, when Johnston scored again and then, in Cyprus, there was the biggest scare of all. Johnston and Richard Gough had scored twice in the game but as time ran out the tie was heading for a 2–2 draw and a disaster. The time-wasting of the Cypriots had been something which concerned Roxburgh before the game and he had stressed to the referee that he must be aware of this element. Never has a warning been taken so much to heart by a match official and never has one been so crucial to the Scottish cause.

As the Cyprus support whistled for full time and as the game moved on minute after minute into injury time, Roy Aitken took a throw-in and hurled the ball into the opposing penalty box where Gough rose, reached it and gave Scotland the winner which would ultimately prove to be the goal which meant most of all in the group games. The time was 97 minutes and the Scottish team had problems getting back to their bus as angry Cypriots surrounded the dressing-room area. For once, luck had favoured Scotland in the tournament, especially as earlier the French – favourites to win the section – had already dropped a point on the tiny Mediterranean island.

Although Scotland lost to Yugoslavia and France away from home, it did not matter. They were even able to drop a point against the Norwegians at Hampden in the final match and still go through. It was a qualifying period which had been dominated by Mo Johnston – who scored in five of the group games and had a tally of six goals from the eight matches. It was an astonishing display of consistent finishing by the striker.

It is little wonder that even today you can hear the present team manager talk longingly of the days when the nation had such men as Johnston and McCoist available for the main striking positions. That is a luxury Craig Brown has not been afforded since he took over.

Target Italy had been achieved and once more the Scots found themselves in a section with Brazil, after a spectacular draw ceremony in Rome. Also there among the four-country group were Sweden and Costa Rica. Once more the off-field problems, which had seemed a distant fading memory, loomed in the fashionable resort of Rapallo where the Scots set up their training headquarters. Immediately after the draw, the Scottish delegation had left on a private jet for Rapallo and booked the Bristol Hotel for the team – the lessons of Mexico had been taken on board. There could be no complaints about *this* hotel, nor about the facilities which were on hand.

However, after a shock defeat from Costa Rica, the supposed minnows of the group – why does that happen so often to Scotland? – things began to fall apart. The result in Genoa had seen Richard Gough limp from the field and 24 hours later being sent home suffering from injury. This compounded an earlier call-off when the late Davie Cooper had pulled out of the squad during the special pre-tournament training in Malta. Then, as Scotland reeled from the Gough injury, two of the players were pictured out on the town when a curfew was supposed to be in force at the team hotel. There were attempts at a cover-up but the pictorial evidence showed one of the players swigging out of a champagne bottle in the street while the other watched.

The Scottish Football Association had warned the team that this type of misbehaviour would not be tolerated by the local authorities nor by the Association's own security officer. A hastily assembled press conference the next day tried to defuse the situation, but the pictures spoke volumes and the attempts at damage-limitation failed. Threats of legal action, too, were never followed through and the players and the coaching staff knew that they now had to do their talking on the park.

To their credit they did so when, in the second game in Genoa, they defeated Sweden 2–1 with goals from Stuart McCall and, inevitably, Mo Johnston. Now there was hope that the team could make that extra stride forward, although Brazil lay in wait at the Stadio Dell Alpe at Turin four days later. There the Scots lost 1–0 – unluckily it has to be said – and eight years later in Miami the Brazilian keeper Taffarel admitted as much when he cast his mind back to a late save he made from Johnston that night. But he saved and Brazil survived that late-goal attempt and Scotland had to wait another 24 hours before their fate was sealed and they knew that, once more, they were en route to Glasgow thinking over what might have been if only they had not failed against Costa Rica, if only Johnston's shot had beaten the Brazilian keeper, if only other results had gone in their favour. It was the same old litany and one which was not any the less saddening because of its ever-increasing familiarity. Next time round, however, the disappointment, the trauma, the heartbreak, the raising of hopes only to have them dashed again, were not there. Scotland did not get to the United States in 1994 after a dismal attempt at qualifying for the finals.

In ten qualifying games the Scots were able to win only four – and those were against Estonia and Malta. Against the important teams, those nations they knew they must defeat if they were to get to the States, they flopped woefully. From the first game in Berne, where they surrendered 3–1 to the Swiss, through a five-goal thrashing from Portugal in Lisbon and a 3–1 loss to Italy in Rome, the team was in tatters. Nor were they able to win any of their home games against these three countries. They drew 0–0 with both the Portuguese and the Italians and then 1–1 with Switzerland and after that game Andy Roxburgh announced that he was quitting, both as team manager and as national coach. He had successfully taken the team to the European Championships in Sweden a year earlier, but now he had failed in the big one, failed in the main event, and he must have felt that after seven years his time was up.

For those of us who did cover the finals in the States it was something of a relief to know that the roller-coaster of emotions which comes as an essential piece of baggage with any Scotland team at the event was absent this time. And yet, and yet . . . I missed that and I missed the fans who add that special unique colour to the tournament, and I believe that the finals missed the Tartan Army's contribution!

That was why it was so good to be back on familiar ground in France last summer when Scotland were back among the world's élite and all the depressingly familiar tragedies followed the team, and still the fans made friends as only they can do and for a day or two the French capital was turned into a tartan wonderland as even Paris realised something special was happening.

I

Qualification '98

With the qualifying sequence broken – and while everyone has become obsessed by the fact that Scotland have yet to reach the second stage of the finals in all their years of trying – it is perhaps worth noting that to get to the finals on five successive occasions is a cause for celebration in itself. Any nation of comparable size would be happy with that.

The disappointment, though, which followed the game against Switzerland at Pittodrie, when failure was made certain, ran deep. The supporters, who were now used to their excursions to the finals every four years, were in despair. It was all the harder for them to bear as they had all felt that they would be able to march forward as they always seemed to have done. None of them seriously expected the team to top the group – after all, the Italians were there to do that – but they visualised a second-place spot for Scotland ahead of Switzerland – who had not been at the finals since England in 1966.

That was not to be, however, and when the Swiss clinched their place and Andy Roxburgh stepped aside for the top coaching job with the Union of European Football Associations, then it was time, once more, for a new beginning.

Again, the SFA ignored the demands from the supporters for a glamorous appointment. It was not something they seriously considered as name after name was put forward in tabloid polls. They had identified the man they wanted. Just as with Andy Roxburgh in 1986, the Association looked towards its own staff.

The man who had been Roxburgh's right-hand man throughout his reign was there after all. Craig Brown, who had collected experience of the World Cup finals in 1986 in Mexico – when Alex Ferguson had chosen him as part of the backroom staff –

then the finals in Italy and the European Championships in Sweden in 1992, was appointed.

Brown, who had had club experience with Motherwell and Clyde and whose promising career as a player had been damaged because of a knee injury, stepped into the same situation as his friend and predecessor Roxburgh had done. The fans looked at his CV and then compared it unfavourably with that of Alex Ferguson and Kenny Dalglish and others. Brown did not possess the aura which the fans wanted the team manager to have, but he provided continuity – always important when the reins are being handed over from one team boss to another. That, as well as his coaching credentials, convinced the men at Park Gardens that they should not look beyond him. Brown was, therefore, put in charge for the last two qualifying games, in Rome and in Malta, games where he could find his feet and establish his authority. He did that in Rome when he dropped the Celtic midfield star and captain Paul McStay from the team. It was almost as if he was making a declaration there and then that he was going to be his own man, no matter how long he had been associated with Andy Roxburgh and the squad.

Like Roxburgh before him, Brown knew that changes had to be made to the squad, that some players had to be moved on and fresh players brought in and, gradually, as the months passed he placed his own stamp on the selection, working towards a tactical set-up which he was convinced Scotland had to adopt to be successful.

He looked around Europe, he studied the defensive formations used by different teams there and he decided that he must play with three central defenders, a system which had been tried by the late Jock Stein many years before and abandoned after the players failed to settle into new ways. Brown knew that. He knew, too, that British players are notoriously sceptical of change: real, meaningful change. The new man, though, was convinced that this was the way forward for Scotland, that this was, indeed, what was required to rebuild the confidence of the squad after the disastrous qualifying period, and to allow a safety-net for these players who were coming in and were new to the international scene.

Brown also reckoned that he had players who would fit comfortably into the formation he wanted and so Colin Calderwood and Colin Hendry were to become the cornerstone of his team. Hendry was relatively untried when Brown took over and Calderwood was previously 'uncapped'. Soon others began to follow as Brown altered the squad substantially. Tosh McKinlay appeared as well as Billy McKinlay. And then Craig Burley, Paul Lambert, Darren Jackson and Jackie McNamara joined the squad.

There were times Brown was accused of being too conservative in his selections, of failing to bring in enough new faces, but the personnel of his squads differed radically from those selected by Roxburgh and throughout his time in the position he has tried as far as possible to allow new players a chance. The squad which went to France contained 14 out of 22 players who had all been handed their first honours by him. Before France and 1998, however, there was Euro '96.

Brown guided the team – by now, *his* team – to the European Championships – which were being held in England – and was close to finding further success there but, as with other team managers before him, he expected to be judged on the qualifying matches in the World Cup. The scrutiny this time round would be even more severe than usual after the way the team had flopped prior to the 1994 finals.

When the groups were drawn, Brown found that the Scots had been placed with Sweden, who had finished third in the tournament in the States and who still had the nucleus of that team available to the manager, Tommy Svensson; Austria; and a clutch of lesser-known, but potentially awkward, opponents in Estonia and Latvia from the Baltic States, their near neighbours Belarus and the remote Faroe Islands.

The Swedes, mightily impressive in the 1994 tournament, were clear favourites to take the section, and Brown began to assess his own team's chances in terms of second position and a possible play-off. He was not being pessimistic in doing so, he was taking the realist's view of the situation which confronted him and second position appeared to be the best option. After the draw, Brown began to calculate points totals and, for his own team, he was remarkably accurate.

There was only one situation where he got things seriously wrong and that was in his estimation of Sweden. In some ways they lived up to all he had said about them with their performances, but when it came to getting results they slumped. The Scottish support saw that for themselves in the third match

Scotland played in Group Four. Before Sweden arrived for the match at Ibrox, the Scots had opened with an away draw against Austria. In the Ernst Happel Stadium in Vienna, Scotland earned a more than creditable 0–0 scoreline against the Austrians – and, indeed, with a little more self-belief they might have been able to return home with a win. Following that, there was a victory in Riga where Latvia went down to goals from John Collins and Darren Jackson, and then a few days later came the Estonian farce which preceded the first home game against the team Brown had installed as favourites to get to France.

No one who was in Estonia will ever forget the extraordinary events which took place there on that October afternoon . . . and the drama which had begun to enfold the previous night when Scotland went to the local stadium for the official training session allowed to all visiting teams at the same time as the kick-off would be on the next day. It was then that Craig Brown saw the strange mobile platforms which held the floodlights to be used for the match. To say it caused him some anxiety is to underestimate his reaction. The goalkeepers had problems and when the lights were measured they were found to be less than the required power for international matches. The Estonians maintained that the lights had been especially flown in from abroad, that they were happy with them and that the game must take place at the scheduled time which, as it would be dark, would involve using the makeshift apparatus.

The Scots opposed this and asked that the match be switched forward by two hours thus allowing it to be played in daylight. This plea was upheld by the FIFA observer from Luxembourg, but the Estonian FA were adamant that everything was in order and refused to accept that ruling even though the official was within his rights as FIFA's man-on-the-spot.

He had the power to make them comply, but it was only after an exchange of telex messages with FIFA's headquarters in Zurich that what appeared to be the final judgement on the matter was reached. The kick-off was altered and the two countries were informed of the change. Scotland's officials sent the equivalent of the 'Fiery Cross' around the bars and restaurants and hotel of the Estonian capital, Tallinn, to inform the Tartan Army of the new time. But, throughout the morning, rumours spread in the city that Estonia's Icelandic coach, Teitfur Thordarsson, was preparing to ignore the FIFA order. The team was based an hour and a half outside the city and he claimed it would not be possible for him to conclude his preparations properly to be at the stadium at the new time. Meanwhile, at the Scotland headquarters, Brown hurriedly rearranged his training and meal schedules for the day, reorganised transport – which became a major obstacle as the Estonians were far from accommodating – and had his players at the stadium over an hour before the new starting time.

As the minutes ticked away everyone looked at the approach road to the ground waiting for the first glimpse of the Estonian team bus. By now, unofficial word had reached the FIFA observer, the Yugoslav referee and the SFA officials and players that the other team were not coming.

Scotland were given instructions on what had to happen. They took the field as usual, they warmed up as usual, the referee and linesmen checked the goal nets as usual and the Tartan Army cheered the team as usual. Then came the farcical sight of the Scots kicking off with no opposing team on the field of play.

Not only that, but John Collins, captain for the day, then had to move forward and formally place the ball into the empty net to satisfy FIFA requirements on this type of issue. The referee then blew his whistle to end the few minutes of nonsense, the Tartan Army celebrated and sang 'There's only one team in Tallinn' and then they went back to the bars and restaurants they had been pulled away from and the players left the field to return to the dressing-room. It was, even by Scotland's World Cup standards, a bizarre occurrence and even stranger things were to happen. The Scotland team bus left the stadium and while we were filing stories back to our newspapers, the Estonian team bus came into view, drove into the now deserted stadium and their players got themselves ready to play the game at the original kick-off time. Of course, they had no match officials to ratify their appearance and, in any case, the FIFA rule book was clear on the matter. The game would be awarded to Scotland by a 2–0 margin and that gave Craig Brown's team six points out of seven as they approached the crunch game with Sweden at Ibrox in five weeks' time. Or so we all thought.

Then, somehow, in the corridors of power in Zurich, suggestions were being made that the Estonians should be given another chance, that the action taken had been too hasty and that Scotland should not be awarded the game after all. The Estonian FA made a formal protest and when it was heard the initial judgement of FIFA, made according to the rules governing the World Cup competition, was put aside. Instead, Scotland were told that they would have to play the game at a neutral venue and the haggling began all over again until the two countries agreed.

There had been no reasonable explanation for the *volte-face* performed by the game's world rulers. Sympathy for a smaller nation is one which has been put forward, but you then have to ask yourself if Scotland had failed to appear for a game against, say, Italy or Germany, if any excuses would have been accepted, the answer is obvious and, of course, everyone was left wondering if Lennart Johansson, the Swede who is president of UEFA and who was also a vice-president of FIFA, had any influence in the matter – albeit even indirectly.

The decision meant that Scotland had not been able to draw further away from their rivals at the top of the group and with the replay being ordered, Scotland's influential skipper Gary McAllister, suspended for the initial game in Tallinn, would now miss the Ibrox game against the Swedes. So, Mr Johansson's country benefited greatly from the controversial decision.

What they did not do, though, was benefit from the game itself. Even though they often outplayed Scotland, a goal from John McGinlay after only eight minutes was enough to give Brown's men their second win in the group and allow them to retain their unbeaten record and continue at the top of the six-country table.

The Estonian game, though, would return to haunt the team. The Baltic country wanted the tie replayed in Cyprus, where they had set up a winter training camp because of the desperate sub-zero conditions in their own country. That was rejected by Scotland and finally FIFA alighted on Monaco as their choice of venue for a February date – a date with disaster as far as the Scotland players were concerned. They could only draw 0–0 in the Stade Louis II and the fans bayed their disgust after the game.

The Estonian farce had been a blow for Craig Brown in more ways than one. He had taken the team from Riga to Tallinn on the back of an away victory, with confidence high and a belief among the players that they could build on that result against Latvia. Then came the interruption and the controversy and, while there was the win over the Swedes as a salve, the performance at Ibrox had not been convincing.

Later, Brown was to admit: 'It was not just that the game was put off in Estonia, it was all that went on round about that fixture.

If we had been able to play – but it was impossible given the state of their floodlighting system – then I am sure that we would have won. You could sense that in the mood of the players as they got themselves ready for the game. Then there was disappointment and bewilderment and then the fact that we did not play as well as we might have done against Sweden and when we reached Monaco to play the Estonians there we had gone off the boil a little bit. That happens and it was a hard one for me to take because we had planned the section in a certain way. We had gone over the dates and gone for the dates we felt would suit us best and all the negotiations meant nothing because of the decision going against us after the game had been postponed.'

Brown had wanted to start with Austria and then build towards Sweden by way of two away games on the Baltic and he also wanted to finish with two home games against supposedly weaker opponents. Then came the blip in Tallinn and the best-laid schemes of Brown and the SFA secretary Jim Farry were damaged. Still, the Scottish team, showing minor alterations as it progressed, recovered with two crucial home wins in four days.

At Rugby Park a goal from Tom Boyd and an own goal saw Scotland defeat Estonia 2–0 and then Kevin Gallacher scored twice when Austria were defeated by the same score at Celtic Park. By now Paul Lambert was becoming a fixture in midfield and Christian Dailly was edging his way into the squad.

Brown was doing what he had done before, what he had been forced to do when he took over the job as international team manager: make changes, while not disturbing the team too radically. He took his own time to set up his defensive system, waiting until he had the players available to him who he thought would be comfortable playing in the new-look formation. Now he was still tinkering with the personnel and with the style of play. Lambert was to become a key element *en route* to the finals, sitting in front of the defensive trio and setting up attacks from there, as well as denying opposition attackers space on the edge of the penalty area.

There was a defeat in Stockholm to get over, when the team lost 2–1 with Kevin Gallacher again the scorer, before an end-of-the-season game in Minsk against Belarus. It was a game which had worried Brown from the time the dates were settled, not because of any threat he saw from the Belarus team – they eventually finished bottom of the group – but because of the timing.

He explained: 'Traditionally, we are at our best when our domestic season has just kicked off. The players are fresh, they are fit and they are desperate to be back playing at the top level once more. But there was no other date available for us to play in Minsk. So many of the opposing teams in this particular group had winter shutdowns that our options were limited and we accepted that.

'We had no alternatives really. What I wanted to do was to have a kind of danger-limitation, if you like, by playing one of the weakest teams in the section at a time which was not good for our players. Here we were, at the end of a long, hard season, trying to keep the players fit and have them in the proper frame of mind for a match which we knew would attract only a few thousand supporters. Not easy! We won, though, and a penalty kick from Gary McAllister set us up for the two home matches we had still to play.'

By now Brown was taking stock of the situation and while it seemed that winning the group was still out of Scotland's reach, the possibility of being the best of the second-placed teams grew more and more likely. Brown worked out the various permutations and, as the games against Belarus and then Latvia grew closer, even the ever-cautious team manager was ready to predict that Scotland would miss the play-off hurdle. He was right. A 4–1 win against Belarus, goals from Kevin Gallacher (2) and David Hopkin (2), and then a 2–0 win against the Latvians at Celtic Park when Gallacher, again, and Gordon Durie scored, carried the team into the finals.

Twenty-four hours later I was in France with Brown and other SFA officials as they began to check out possible training headquarters for the summer. The party flew to Lyon where they would commence their search and within a couple of days Brown had settled on the village of St-Rémy-de-Provence and the splendidly equipped Hostellerie du Vallon de Valruegues set in its own grounds at the top of a narrow road leading from the little town which would, in the summer, adopt the Scottish team.

At first it seemed reckless to book the hotel before knowing where the team would be playing the matches, but Brown was sure that at least one of them would be in the region, whether at Marseille, Lyon or St-Etienne. Again he was right, with St-Etienne being the final group-game venue for the Scots when the draw was made.

In any case, as he stressed: 'The way the French organisers and FIFA have planned this World Cup, travelling for fairly long distances is something which just about every team will have to do at some time or another. They planned it so that the teams could be seen in different regions and, so, no matter where we stay we shall be forced into awkward journeys.

'In any case we want to be based where the temperatures are high. Our medical people believe that it is best for our players. One, or maybe even two, of the games will be played in the heat and we will be properly acclimatised for that. But, also, having trained in the heat we shall benefit in terms of stamina if we have to play in cooler conditions. We have worked this out before. Before England in Euro '96 we went to the United States and we worked the lads very hard up in New England where it was hot, and then even harder in Florida where the temperatures were up in the 80s and 90s and in all three games we played there we finished up stronger than the opposition. That is why we shall be doing this again. It's something which we have found benefits the players and we want to have any advantage that we can in this tournament, believe me. We shall be as fit as any country at these finals. We won't be leaving anything to chance whatsoever.'

All of those matters were talked through carefully.

Brown continued: 'The medical people have their own views on the matter and then the rest of the backroom staff have their say and we talk it through with some of the squad members as well. These matters may look inconsequential, but they are not. In a longish campaign we have to try to make sure that we look at all the different aspects of the preparation. You have to have the players fit and you have to have them comfortable in their environment and you have to try to make sure that they are going to be peaking at the right time. If you peak too soon in terms of general fitness then some of the work everyone has put in can be wasted.'

Brown had made his hotel choice – beating the Italians to it – and he had visited other venues where he had selected hotels which would be used as stop-overs for the matches. Now all he awaited was the draw in Marseille to find out his – and the country's – fate.

On Saturday, 6 December, the die was cast and Craig Brown found himself in charge of the biggest-ever game Scotland had been asked to play in. The draw had paired them with the world champions Brazil in the opening game of the tournament and also put them in the same group as Norway and Morocco – two countries who were very much higher in the FIFA rankings than Brown's side. And yet, and yet, this was at least practically the news the Tartan Army had wanted. Brazil again! The sequence of playing against Brazil in every single finals that had been played in Europe since 1974 was continuing. One draw and two defeats so far was the saddening statistic from the fixtures held in West Germany, Spain and Italy, but the supporters did not care too greatly about that. Just to see the Brazilians, to go to the opening game, to be a part of it all, that was going to be enough. The plans to see the match started to be made all around the country, while Brown also took to the road to finalise hotels in France and then to watch Brazil in a tournament in Miami and to see Norway face France back in Marseille.

Brown knew, though, the strengths of the teams he was now asked to tackle. What he did not know until he reached Miami was the turmoil within the South American squad with the veteran team manager Mario Zagallo already coming under fire and then – after the results in the CONCACAF Gold Cup tournament – discovering when he arrived back in Rio, that the public were asking for him to be sacked and that the Federation had appointed Zico to a position as his number two, even though Zagallo had insisted that he required no help from the former international player.

It was not the confident Brazilians thar we had expected to see in the United States, undistinguished displays against Jamaica and Guatemala and then a defeat from the United States when they moved to the tourney's later stages in Los Angeles, gave Brown a new insight on the team he had watched winning the World Cup in the same country four years earlier. But he was not totally taken in by the signs of unrest and the lack of form shown by some of the players.

'They are missing a few lads here,' he said. 'Dunga, who is very influential, is in Japan with his club, and Ronaldo isn't here nor Roberto Carlos, and so we have to balance all of that. And, in my view, Zagallo will get things right because he has been over this course so often before. More than any other coach who will be in France in the summer. And he knows the value of having the squad ready for the summer and not for some smaller event such as this.

'I would have expected them to show more than they have done, but it was important to take a look at them and to see just how they are playing as a unit. That won't alter too much, the basic structure of the team, though the individuals will change.'

The Brazilian 0–0 draw with Jamaica followed by the 1–1 result against tiny Guatemala brought the wrath of the large emigrant Brazilian population in Florida down on Zagallo's head as he escaped after the second game to the haven of the ultra-luxurious Biltmore Hotel, where they were based. Before reaching the bus the coach had to run a gauntlet of furious fans outside the dressing-room entrance of the Orange Bowl. And, as he left with cries for his resignation ringing around the stadium carparks, inside the stadium the scene was vastly different as the Guatemalan team captain accepted a call from the country's President congratulating him and the team on the finest result in the nation's history. The player stood to attention when he discovered who was on the other end of the phone during the after-match press conference and that brought it home to everyone there just how highly esteemed the Brazilians remained – even though their own supporters were so very, very disappointed at what the players had shown. Even the new star, Denilson, was unimpressive, and there was little to support Zagallo as he attempted a spirited defence of his selection and his tactics. His was a voice crying in the wilderness and with the problems growing behind the scenes and with Scotland being asked to play them in the opening game there was some reason for optimism. Not a heady over-optimistic view that Scotland might get a victory against the South Americans; more of a rational look at the situation with the very obvious fact that opening games were almost always close-run affairs and frequently ended in a draw. And with Zagallo and Zico set to bicker over the team, and maybe even over the tactics, then that type of diversion could only bring succour to the opposition – in this case Scotland.

Brown did subscribe a little to the opening-game theory, but he refused to accept that Mario Zagallo, with his World Cup record, would fail to haul the world champions back to the stunning brilliance they had shown in the United States when they triumphed in the 1994 final. If any country realised the need to peak at the correct time for the tournament then, Brown reasoned, it had to be Brazil. And so, while there was hope as he went about his planning, there was also a strong sense of realism from Brown.

He knew that, as well as watching opponents, he had to keep his own players active. There were midweek gaps in the club fixture lists which allowed him to slot in matches and he did so. Indeed, on his initial fact-finding mission to France, he had accepted at short notice a match against the host nation in the Geoffrey Guichard Stadium in St-Etienne. The team lost 2–1 to a late penalty from Youri Djorkaeff but Rangers' Gordon Durie scored a first-half equaliser when the team had gone behind and Brown was pleased with the display, and especially pleased when the draw was made that the players had been able to experience the atmosphere at the stadium where they were set to meet Morocco.

Following that, Brown organised two games at home. The first was in March against Denmark and Scotland lost to a Brian Laudrup goal. That game was at Ibrox, and the next took place a month later at Easter Road where Brown's men could only manage a 1–1 draw with Finland. The Scots went behind to a goal from Rangers' Jonathan Johansson and then equalised a couple of minutes later through Darren Jackson. The team manager was able to experiment a little in each of the games and refused to be downhearted at either of the results.

He explained patiently: 'I could have chosen easy games and in that way we could have gained a couple of wins and everyone would have examined the quality of the opposition and decided that we were not really learning anything.

'This way, we played the Danes, who are among the leading European sides, and Finland, who only just failed to qualify for the finals. So we had true tests and we were also able to try out one or two things and give some of the players that little bit more experience against foreign opposition that is essential when you are approaching the finals of the World Cup.

'Obviously, it would have been tremendous if we had been able to win the games but we didn't. What we did do was lose to Denmark by the only goal of the game and to draw with Finland. And I needed the games and I did not want to go for some easy option.'

Neither of the results – nor that defeat from the French – were liable to send Scotland soaring upwards in the FIFA rankings – that contentious list which is drawn up in Zurich and which so few people seem to understand fully. But Brown did not care about that. He was looking at the broader picture, at the finals and how the team would do there. Which is why, once again, Scotland crossed the Atlantic for two more warm-up games.

II

A Sudden Farewell from 'The Goalie'

By the time the games in the United States loomed, the skipper for the qualifying games, Coventry's midfield player Gary McAllister, had been forced to abandon all hopes of playing in France because of injury. It seemed certain to those outside the training camp that the natural successor to McAllister was the Blackburn Rovers centre-half Colin Hendry. He had the presence, he had also held down the job before, and to the Tartan Army he was their very own 'Braveheart'.

However, for whatever reasons, Craig Brown initially refused to name the man who would wear the captain's armband in the finals. Gradually, though – particularly when the squad flew to Newark a few days after the Scottish Cup final – the odds on Hendry were shortening. The blond central defender who had travelled to see the team against Belarus when he was injured and took his place in the stand with the country's fans, was the man who was chosen for the tough games in the States and for the finals. The two matches organised by Brown were difficult. He had followed the same instincts which had led him to choose Denmark and Finland for the awkward home fixtures.

As with the Danes, Brown chose two teams who would also be playing in the finals, the United States team, of course, and, from South America, Colombia, who were to be in England's qualifying section the following month. The first match was only a few days after the team landed and it was played out at the New York Giants' stadium at the Meadowlands complex in New Jersey.

It was also where the Scots would play the South Americans while the second match a week later was set for the RFK Stadium in Washington DC. It was to be a major farewell for the US team whose group game against Iran had captured the imagination of the American public because of its obvious political implications.

Brown had consulted his players before taking the games in the States as he attempted to find them the proper environment for the final weeks before they headed to France. Twice before, ahead of major tournament finals, the Scots had taken the transatlantic route and on each occasion the team had been comfortable and the backroom staff happy at the hard work which had been put in on the training ground. In advance of the European Championships in Sweden in 1992, Scotland had travelled to Chicago for intensive preparations and then played the USA in Denver and Canada in Toronto. Four years later, prior to England and Euro '96 they had taken the same route, only this time they had played the USA in Hartford, Connecticut and Colombia – the same opposition as was now lined up – in Miami.

Brown explained: 'It is important to take the players away somewhere and allow them to get together as a squad, to work together and eat together and to live together. It's also good to have them some place where they can relax and where the food and the hotels will be to their liking. You never find a problem in either of these areas in the States. Also there is no extra pressure on the players from supporters – okay, you get a few exiled Scots who will turn up at the hotel, but that is always something you can handle. It's not a major worry at all.

'Whereas at home they would be pestered for tickets all the time and we would not be guaranteed the kind of heat training which we want. The States is best. There's no doubt about that. Also we get two games against a couple of countries who are also going to be at the finals which confirms their class. Everything is as we like it and the training facilities you get are always superb.'

So there was the answer for the sniping comments which came out of Norway as the usual propaganda war began to gather force. From Oslo we were being told that the Scots were making a major mistake taking their players so far away when the Norway team manager Egil Olsen was happy to gather his players around him in their own country and play warm-up matches there. Olsen was reported as saying: 'To take players away for long distances so soon before playing in the World Cup is a mistake which we would not make. I can see no point in doing this. Players are better at home and that is why we have decided to remain in Norway. It will pay off for the team in the long run.

When we get to France then people can compare the two sets of players and make their judgements. Trailing halfway across the world tires players.'

Of course, Olsen's needs were somewhat different from Brown's, in the sense that most of his players were playing professionally in other countries in Europe – with a huge percentage in England. To combat his own problems for a get-together, the eccentric Olsen had been forced to travel to Blackburn Rovers' training ground to ensure that he could have all his players around him. Going home was probably important to them, because they spent all their working time away from their native land. The criticism did not faze Brown because he knew what he wanted and what he needed.

Firstly, he wanted to work his men in high temperatures. Secondly, he wanted the team to play in similar conditions to those they would find in France and, in that way, build their stamina for what lay ahead. It had worked for him two years before – he still pointed out how his team had finished fresher than any of the opposing sides in Euro '96 – and it had worked for his predecessor Andy Roxburgh in Sweden in the European Championship four years earlier. That, allied to the strongly held convictions of the medical advisers, was enough to carry the day, no matter what anyone else might say. The Scottish squad based themselves at Short Hills and were working the day after arrival, readying themselves for the Saturday match against the Colombians, knowing that just as they were gaining experience of South American football before the Brazil opener the Colombians were on the same mission. They wanted to get a taste of typically British football to ready themselves for their own game against England.

The trouble for them, however, was that Brown and his coaching staff had been hard at work with the players perfecting the passing game, the possession game that he was determined to use at the finals. What Colombia had to counter was not 'typically British' at all. It was based on what was essentially a European style with Brown adding flavours of his own to the general mix. And it worked. It worked so well, in fact, that there were occasions when the huge Colombian turn-out were joining the Scottish exiles in applauding Brown's players as they passed and passed and passed again and, on more than one occasion, simply did not give the South Americans a glimpse of possession. Yet

Scotland had a dreadful start when they had a penalty awarded against them and Carlos Valderrama, the Colombian veteran, scored. He struck the ball confidently past Wimbledon's Neil Sullivan, the goalkeeper Brown had chosen to allow him some experience in case he was required in France. The goal came in 21 minutes and while the Scots protested the American referee waved them aside and the kick was given and the Scots appeared to be up against it in the sultry heat of the New York night. Then the game began to run Scotland's way as the players settled to their passing game and gradually took control, and before half-time they were in command after goals, glorious goals, too, from John Collins and then Craig Burley pushed them into the lead.

It was now the kind of game the Scottish exiles from all over the country, and from Canada too, had come to see. Scotland gave as cohesive a performance as they had ever done under Brown's rule. There had been other good displays, but few which carried the class, and eventually the confidence, that this one did. When Rincon equalised 12 minutes from the end it was a blow the Scottish players did not deserve. They had done everything Brown had asked of them, and possibly even more, and the portents for France were good.

The players were happy with the new style of play. Brown was delighted that his planning had been executed so professionally by the men under his command and he pointed out: 'The lads did tire a little bit, which was to be expected. We got here on Wednesday and played on the Saturday night and we always reckoned that would be a little bit of a problem having to play without enough time to become acclimatised to the time change and the heat. But it was the way they played for most of the match, and the way they came back after going behind, which was impressive.

'And, again, we were able to have a look at the players who have not been around the squad as long as some of the others. Christian Dailly was very impressive in the wide position on the left where we used him and that is encouraging.'

Dailly, whose career had been, if not blighted then certainly damaged a little, because of his versatility, was also happy enough to be played out of position. While he had settled into the central defensive role with Derby County he had been used to shuttling around between attack and defence during his years of apprenticeship at Dundee United. He said: 'You are looking at the opportunity of playing in the finals of the World Cup next month and that is what counts most. That is something you dream about where you are going to be playing.

'I don't mind where I am asked to play for Scotland. I am happy playing at the centre of defence with Derby and it has been a long, settled run there, but if the team manager believes I can do a job for the team in the role I filled against Colombia, or any other role, then I shall play in it quite happily. Honestly, it is not a concern now and it's not going to be a concern. Scotland and the games in France are what matter most to all of us who are here in the squad. I did think the team played well against the Colombians, and they are a very talented team, so that is encouraging. It allowed us to see how South Americans play, although we all know that there is a difference between them and Brazil. But every little bit of experience helps right now.'

At the team hotel there was that same satisfaction among the squad over the next few days, as articulated by Craig Brown and Dailly.

Then, a few days later, things altered dramatically when those old familiar World Cup gremlins struck Brown's meticulous planning: goalkeeper Andy Gorman decided to leave the squad and return home to deal with what he described as 'fabricated stories' in the tabloid press back in Scotland. On the day he made his decision – and he enlarged that by declaring that he was retiring from international football – the goalkeeper called me aside at the team's hotel before the squad was leaving for a morning work-out. Initially, I thought he was about to tell me that he would meet me in Manhattan the following day when the team was to be given a day off. Instead, he handed me an envelope and explained: 'I gave the letter in this envelope to Craig Brown this morning and this is a copy for you. I have had enough of the tabloids. They are making up stories about me and it's going to upset the entire squad if I stay here. They just won't leave me alone and it is now affecting friends of mine back in Scotland.

'I have had phone calls constantly here at the hotel and it has all become too much. I can't concentrate properly on the game and I feel really concerned that I shall let Scotland down and the rest of the squad down, too, if I don't leave now. I don't want to do this – but they are leaving me no alternative.'

Standing outside the hotel it was difficult to grasp that the player, one of the best Scotland keepers of all time, was about to destroy his international career and the opportunity to find himself a new club now that he was being allowed to leave Rangers. I attempted to reason with him, advising that he should ride out the storm and stay with the squad and go on to France where he might have the chance to impress leading clubs and, perhaps, secure his soccer future. Nothing would sway him. He said: 'I spoke to Craig and he asked me to stay on, but I can't. I handed him the letter at breakfast and then he came to see me and discuss the decision but I told him that it is something that I just have to do. I don't want to see all the preparations being wrecked because of a tabloid circus. Incidentally, I don't want anyone else to know just yet. I want to get myself away on a plane without being tracked by news reporters. The only people who know, so far, are Craig, yourself and Gordon Durie because he is my room-mate and he has suffered by being wakened in the middle of the night by these calls I have been getting. I can't let this go on.'

It was clear that Goram was not for turning on the issue. He left to make his flight arrangements for the return journey. Later the Scotland team manager insisted: 'I wanted him to stay on – but he had this in his mind that his presence here was going to cause problems for the other lads and for our World Cup preparations. He was adamant that only by leaving could he guarantee that the squad would not suffer from whatever was going on back home. He was genuinely upset when he talked things over with me. This was after I had read the letter and I had hoped, then, to talk him round. But I think the fact that he had written the letter before we spoke told its own story. He had his mind made up.'

His Rangers team-mate Gordon Durie added revealingly: 'With Andy there are times when you know that he is not going to change his mind on an issue. This was one of these times. He would not budge. He told me he was going to give Craig the letter and when I said he should think about it again he told me he had done so. And he felt the only way he could get peace of mind was by flying back home and dealing with the problems which existed there.

'He believed the only way to handle the aggro he was getting from the tabloids was to get back home and try to sort things out there. I think the fact that we were so far from home and, also, we had until the following weekend before we would be back was worrying him. He just wanted to go straightaway. And he did.'

While the other players went to a training session, Goram was packing and making his way to Newark Airport for the return flight. He did not even say goodbye to the others for fear of causing more upset. Nor did he talk to his goalkeeping guru Alan Hodgkinson who had nurtured his career at the club and country level over the years and who had enthused over the way the keeper was working in the training sessions which had been held. The injury worries he had nursed towards the end of the season had disappeared. Hodgkinson was to tell me later: 'He looked better than I have ever seen him. And he was working harder than he had ever done. All the lads were talking about how well he looked and the amount of really hard graft he was putting in. I just wish he had talked to me and I might have been able to convince him to stay. I know that Andy can be stubborn and this might have been one of these occasions when he would listen to no one.'

I did not open the envelope and read the letter until I was back in Manhattan – as per his instructions. The note was explicit and, as the man they call 'The Goalie' had explained, it spelled out his decision and his concerns about the upset which could be caused to the international squad's pre-World Cup training. It was handwritten and it read as follows:

It's plain to see that stories are being fabricated to upset me or our World Cup preparations. Myself, Craig Brown and the players don't need this!! It's a very important time of people's lives.

Players are ready to give everything for their country. I am now 'clubless' and need to organise my future. The last thing the squad needs is controversy off the park. They have an objective, they don't want anything to divert their focus on what really matters – the World Cup.

Yes, you have got to me! [Press] But I won't let it upset Craig's plans. If anything you have made his job easier!

It would be easier for me to just sit and collect my money for participating, as a player or substitute, from the World Cup and the players' pool . . . money doesn't come into it. I've never played in a World Cup, but contentment is more important than controversy.

From today, Thursday, 26 June, I've retired from international football. I'd like to thank Alex Ferguson for giving me the opportunity to play for Scotland. Andy and Craig for continuing to select me, it's been a memorable 12 years!!

It's a very difficult decision but it's in the interest of everybody involved.

I'd like to take this opportunity to wish Craig, Alex, all the backroom staff, Jim Leighton, Neil Sullivan and last but not least Hodgy . . . all the very best for the World Cup and their futures in football.

Best wishes,

Andy Goram

And so, in fewer than 300 words, Andy Goram wrote his own international epitaph just at a time when it seemed that he would be handed the number one goalkeeping spot for his country in the World Cup finals. He had edged himself ahead of Jim Leighton – but only just – at Euro '96 and the way he was working so impressively in training suggested that the decision could have gone the same way once more. In the thousands of words which followed the story breaking few seemed to appreciate the sacrifice Goram was making. 'I've never played in a World Cup,' he wrote, and in these seven words 'The Goalie' encapsulated how difficult the decision had been for him. Eight years earlier he had thought he had a chance of playing following the agonies Jim Leighton suffered at Manchester United when he was axed for the FA Cup final replay, but it was snatched away from him. Then for USA '94 the team had not qualified. France was his last chance – and he walked away from it to take the heat off the team manager and the players he would have shared that experience with. At the team hotel, of course, life went on. Brown handled a prickly press conference well and carried on with his preparations, calling in Celtic goalkeeper Jonathan Gould to take up the third keeper's position, and then proceeded to select a team for the second tour game against the United States. Jim Leighton was selected and Brown admitted that the side which finished the game would be very close to that which would begin the World Cup against Brazil. Most of the players were still mystified by Goram's sudden departure, but Brown and the backroom staff soon had them refocused on the job in hand. And the hope the manager expressed – for high temperatures – was granted.

It had been hot in New York, but moving down to Washington saw the temperature soar towards one hundred degrees, with a humidity which was unbearable. The players felt the difference in training, but at the stadium itself when the game was staged on the Saturday afternoon they found themselves in an atmosphere which drained them of strength and stamina. Yet again they showed the style they had demonstrated against Colombia, persevering with their patient passing game and, while wilting towards the end, still managed to gain a respectable 0–0 draw with a home team who had hoped to give the massive Washington crowd a farewell victory before heading for the finals. Afterwards, some players complained of losing seven to eight pounds in weight in the oven which the RFK Stadium had become. In the shade the mercury reached over 90 degrees and estimates of the heat on the field took that into the low hundreds. It was what Brown and his medical advisers had looked for as an aid to building stamina and resilience on the tour. To the players' enormous credit they came through the pain barrier which they were forced to suffer and the 0–0 draw was again a result which satisfied Brown in his quest for the proper tactics and the correct personnel to employ in France. It was just ten days later when Scotland would open the greatest soccer show on earth. The two-game trip had been worth while as Brown had forecast, with only the defection of Andy Goram upsetting the plans and even that was now behind the manager and the squad. As Goram had said, they had 'an objective – the World Cup'. The glamour of the Brazilians seen from afar had been exciting enough. Now going into action against the champions of the world was soon to become reality for these players.

It was what they talked about. It was now a constant in their thoughts. They had known since the draw that the television audience was to be the biggest ever known for a football match. They had known the opposition would be favourites to win the trophy once again. But, in between times, they had had their own club careers to concentrate on. There had been titles and cups to be won but now that was over. Now the biggest game of their careers waited for them.

When the match in Washington ended many of the players knew from what Craig Brown had said beforehand that they were now almost certain to be played in the first match in the Stade de France on the outskirts of Paris on 10 June.

The team which finished that match against the United States was: Jim Leighton (Aberdeen); Colin Calderwood (Spurs), Colin Hendry (Blackburn Rovers), Tom Boyd (Celtic); Jackie McNamara (Celtic), Craig Burley (Celtic), Paul Lambert (Celtic), John Collins (Monaco), Christian Dailly (Derby County); Darren Jackson (Celtic) and Kevin Gallacher (Blackburn Rovers).

True to his word, these were the men Brown named in Paris – with the exception that Jackie McNamara stepped aside to allow

Gordon Durie to continue his profitable partnership with Kevin Gallacher up front, one which had been interrupted when the Rangers' front player was injured against Colombia in the Giants' stadium and young Simon Donnelly had taken his place. Yet, between Washington and Paris, Brown had several false leads to set for the Brazilians as the off-field mind games took hold in the days leading up to the big kick-off. It has ever been thus, and Brown with his experience in Mexico and Italy knew that.

III

St-Rémy-de-Provence – and the Phoney War Begins

From the moment you drove into the little tourist town of St-Rémy-de-Provence, population given as just over 9,000, you knew that the presence of the Scotland international team had the population *en fête*. It may be one of the more fashionable centres in Provence – Princess Caroline of Monaco has a home there – but the arrival of Craig Brown and his players saw saltires hung from the windows of private homes and from shops and flutter above the main street, as the residents welcomed their footballing visitors.

The French organisers, including Michel Platini, had hoped that the whole nation would feel involved in the tournament – hence the scattered nature of the matches. In St-Rémy, the Scots helped fulfil the promise made by the one-time French captain and team manager. The people here, caught midway between Marseille and Montpellier where they would watch some of the games, had an interest all of their own. As well as France they could now support Scotland.

The public relations work done by the Scottish Football Association among the townsfolk was impressive. The local schools had competitions involving the tournament, but with a special Scottish accent added. And the freedom afforded the players was better than it had been at previous tournaments. Obviously, at the hotel, just a little way from the town centre, there was a strong security presence at the gates to the grounds. That is part of the price which has to be paid by all competitors at major sports events nowadays. And at the school hall, where Craig Brown held his daily press conferences, the police maintained a group of officers to travel with the Scottish backroom staff and players and had other officers stationed around the hall itself. Similar security measures were taken at the training, even though Brown often allowed the local children into watch the players at work. All of this was absolutely normal, if still a little bit unexpected for those players who had not experienced the full power of security at previous tournaments. But there was an element which was a little different. During the players' rest periods you could see them stroll around the town, signing autographs for the locals, looking at the shops and enjoying a coffee at some of the cafés and restaurants scattered throughout the town. They were allowed that little bit of freedom and it underlined the choice of St-Rémy as a sensible decision by Brown. Unlike some previous occasions there was nothing there that anyone could complain about. The surroundings were idyllic and the weather was as Brown had hoped. Hot. Too hot for many of us, even the locals complained that the temperatures were so much higher than normal for this time of the year. But it was all about reinforcing Brown's theory about the training routines and the effects of working in hot conditions and being able to face any climatic changes much more easily than if you are asked to go from the cold into the heat. He could not have been happier, nor could he have seemed more relaxed as the countdown began and word came from the Brazilian training camp up to the south-east of Paris that Mario Zagallo had already decided on his team.

The ageing, under-pressure coach had announced a month earlier that now Romario was out, his place would be taken by Bebeto, who would slot in alongside Ronaldo up front. He then went through the rest of the team and declared that he saw no need for delaying and the team he had named earlier would play. It was an impressive display of confidence for a man who was still being pilloried by the Brazilian press and public and it was clearly intended to take the pressure away from him as the opening game approached. Also, naturally, it was designed to heap all of the pressure on Brown. In the first signs of the phoney war in France, Zagallo had thrown down the gauntlet attempting to provoke Brown into a reply, hoping, in fact, that the Scotland manager would name his own team and allow Zagallo to lay his plans accordingly.

Of course, when the draw had been made and Brown had travelled to Miami, Zagallo had declared himself disinterested in watching Scotland in any of their planned 'friendlies'. He proclaimed then: 'With Brazil we are not so interested in how the opposition plays as to how we play ourselves. If we play to our full capabilities then that is usually enough to give us victory. All we need is a little knowledge of the other teams – not too much.'

Ahead of the Scotland game, though, Zagallo seemed to know very little about his first-match opponents. He had asked for a video of the games in the United States, and that had not turned up and so now he cursorily named his team and waited for Brown's response. The Scotland manager was too long in the tooth to fall for this ploy, and even when questioned by Brazilian journalists following the Zagallo party-line, Brown had ready answers to deflect them.

On one occasion, at a press briefing on the Sunday before the game, Brown listened to the comments about Zagallo being unprepared as regards his knowledge of the Scotland team and then replied: 'I just don't believe all of that kind of talk for a moment. Every coach does his homework and Mario Zagallo will have done his. It is a part of our jobs.'

Brown had made his studies of the Brazilians but, in spite of Zagallo having named a team a month in advance and then confirming it in France, there were differing strands of thought emanating from a Brazilian camp which seemed split between Zagallo and Zico; between the head coach and the *éminence grise* who had been appointed against his wishes by the Federation.

The turmoil among the Brazilians was in contrast to the peaceful build-up being enjoyed by the Scots. The question was whether it would disrupt the champions in any way before the game. Brown himself did not think so. Nor did any of his players. His view was simple: 'They are a country with perfect attendance at the World Cup finals and if any nation knows how to handle all the pressures which exist then that nation is Brazil. I am not going to pay too much attention to all the reports of trouble in the camp. I am going to concentrate on the team I believe they will field and on my own team and how we can handle this whole thing.

'There is an awful lot of pressure on the lads going into the opener with all the pomp and ceremony which will surround it. What we shall be trying to do is get round them all in the dressing-room, talk to them individually and tell them again what we expect from them, and we have to make sure that they are not hypnotised by those yellow jerseys when they see them.

'They can be worth a goal of a start in some games to the

Brazilians, because the opposition players just freeze when they suddenly come face to face with the best team in the world. Well, we don't want any of our lads to freeze on the night. They have to be ready to do the job and they must try to treat it as just another international, though, having said that, I know as well as everyone else that it is far from that.'

Zagallo's almost sniffy disdain regarding the make-up of the Scotland squad was exaggerated as Brown had thought. At one training session, Brown saw that film crews from Brazil were in operation when this particular work-out had been designated by FIFA as private. The world governing body had decreed that press conferences at all training camps had to be open and that, similarly, a proportion of training sessions should also be public. Others, though, were listed as private, to allow teams to work on set-pieces and to attempt new formations away from the prying gaze of their opponents. This was being abused at the little local stadium in St-Rémy and Brown decided on evasive action to get some of his players away from the hidden cameras.

'It was unbelievable what they got up to,' he laughed, 'and where they placed their cameras so that they could film us without our knowledge. But we had an idea it might happen and we kept our eyes open. Eventually, though, we knew that the one way we would be sure to beat them was to organise a separate training session for selected players, one which would really be private. And that is what we did. We even smuggled the players in question out of the hotel so that they would not be seen heading for another destination. We felt that it was important for us to do this.'

The importance for Brown and Alex Miller and his other coaches lay in their strong belief that many of the goals at the finals would come from set-piece moves. The Scots worked hard on free-kicks, and the manager felt it essential that they might be able to devise one or two fresh moves which would surprise their opponents. Hence the need for secrecy. And so it was that free-kick specialists John Collins, Paul Lambert, Craig Burley and Billy McKinlay were whisked away from the rest of the squad to go through a fresh routine of dead-ball situations, this time far from the prying lenses of the South American spies. Brown revelled in the planning involved and, more particularly, in its success.

As early as the United States he had talked of the value of free-kicks in the modern game and especially when applied to the finals of the World Cup. He knew that every team spent many hours on this aspect of the game, knowing that in highly organised modern-day football, defences are more and more difficult to breach, more and more difficult to get behind, because of the strategies employed by the coaches. Brown was right, of course, and as the finals unfolded it became more and more obvious how vital the set-pieces were. They did bring the majority of the goals in the tournament, and the defences were organised and even the weaker countries were able to put together tactics to frustrate the stronger attacking sides. Naturally there were exceptions to this general rule, but the reality remained that fitness and strength and organisation can stifle the finest and most skilful of teams. Which is why even the Brazilians spend hour after hour on the training ground perfecting their own free-kicks. If that was good enough for the champions then Brown would follow them.

Brown also emphasised that in the absence of Gary McAllister – he was with the squad to add his expertise off the field but still not fit to play – John Collins would be the team's dead-ball expert. Said Brown: 'He will take any penalties we may be awarded, and the free-kicks and even the corners because he is the best player we have for delivering a ball. He knows instinctively when to shoot or when to play the ball to a team-mate. It comes easily to him.'

The countdown had now commenced and yet there was almost an understated feeling in the Scottish training camp, as if they knew a day of destiny had to be faced and they would be ready for whatever eventuality came along. It was as if they had come to terms with the pressures of the opening game and did not feel that anything could now deflect them from the job in hand.

But, while Brown and his players looked comfortable, the hype surrounding Brazil continued. Two days before the game, a Brazilian journalist whom I had met in Miami expressed his concern over the in-fighting at the training camp and insisted that the Brazilian team would not contain several of Zagallo's favoured stars. He assured me that Denilson would not play; that Leonardo would be left on the bench; and that the influence of the Federation president, Ricardo Texeira, being channelled through his man Zico, was behind these moves. The team, he told me, would be Taffarel; Cafu, Junior Baiano, Aldair, Roberto Carlos; Cesar Sampaio, Dunga, Giovani, Rivaldo; Bebeto and Ronaldo.

This was to be the team which started the game against the Scots in the Stade de France, as the squabbling and the back-biting among the backroom staff refused to go away.

The absence of Denilson confirmed that Zagallo had lost total command. He had always spoken highly of the left-sided midfield player and had considered him as his protégé. On several occasions I had declared that if they had played at the same time, that if Denilson, for instance, had been around in 1958 when Zagallo played in the Brazil team which won the trophy in Sweden, then Denilson would have been chosen to play. Yet, here he was sitting out the opening game on the bench, while Rivaldo took his place. Little wonder the Brazilian media were engrossed by the power struggle which was going on within their squad headquarters.

Scotland simply trained as usual, although 48 hours before the game, Brown did not take his place at the daily press conference; he remained at the hotel studying videos of the Brazilians and working on ways to combat their attacking stars. Already he had suggested that the most effective way of handling the Inter Milan striker Ronaldo, the young man who was tipped to be the major star of the tournament, was by cutting off the supply of the ball to him. The £20 million front player had insisted that he wanted to be the Pele of these finals, the biggest star at France '98, and Brown felt he had to have a special strategy to limit his runs at the Scots defence.

'When he has the ball at his feet and sets off on one of those runs then he is a very hard man to stop,' Brown stressed. 'We want to have our midfield stopping him receiving the ball in front of him in the way he likes it best. We want to make our moves in the middle of the field rather than around our own penalty area, and we want to see the lads intercepting passes rather than making tackles. We have to be very aware of the new refereeing rules.

'This is the opening game and it will be the game where FIFA will be insistent that the new strictures about tackling from behind and all the other little adjustments which have been made are brought into force. We have gone over these with the players and talked them through it; when we played the United States we had just 12 fouls given against us in the 90 minutes, so we have players who know how to handle this. What we want to avoid is conceding free-kicks around the penalty box, you only have to look at how Roberto Carlos hits the ball to realise that is a must. But we have lads in the middle of the field who are good at cutting out passes and jockeying players. Paul Lambert is excellent at playing that kind of game. He stands up to players so well, you never see him grounded at all and he will be vital.'

But while Brown fielded the questions on how the Scots were going to stop the might of the Brazilians, the players were talking of having to be able to mount their own attacking moves. The view from them was simple – if they allowed the Brazilians too much room, afforded them too much respect, then there was a danger of becoming little more than cannon fodder for the champions.

Rangers' striker Gordon Durie pointed out: 'We happen to believe that we can surprise them a little bit because all they seem to be doing is talking about how we shall play a typical British-style game. And we won't be doing that at all. The manager and his assistant Alex Miller have been concentrating on the passing game we used in the United States. That is the way they want to see us playing and it is far from being "typically British". If the Brazilians are looking for the long high balls into the penalty box then they will be looking in vain.

'The game where they are more likely to find that, is when they come up against Norway – because that is exactly the way they perform. We have had it preached to us that it is fatal to give the ball away at this level, losing possession is a major sin.

'Anyhow, we have to try to attack them at some stage of the game. It would be suicide to sit back. We have to get forward ourselves and probe away to see if we can find weaknesses in their defence. That might just be possible – whether it is or not we just have to try. If we play as well as we did in the two games in the United States, against Colombia and the States themselves, then we will give them something to think about.'

There was a heartening sense of perspective about the Scots in the build-up and even on the eve of their flight to Paris – the squad travelled north 24 hours before the game to allow training at the Stade de France – the laid-back approach persisted. While Brown closeted himself at the hotel with his team plans and his line-up secrets, his right-hand man Alex Miller was musing over how it would be in the dressing-room before the opening ceremony commenced. It would be quiet, he decided, and that would be exactly what he and Brown would be looking for.

'When there is a quietness about the place, when the lads are that little bit subdued before the kick-off,' he explained, 'then you know that they are looking at the game already. They are focusing on the jobs they have been asked to do. I can sense that there is an edge on them now. It has been there at training and also around the hotel and I am convinced that it will still be with them in the Stade de France. Look, we are going to be the underdogs before the game starts and we know that is how it is.

'The people at the game, the other countries who are here, the worldwide television audience will all be expecting the Brazilians to win. We shall be written off, but that is how we like it. There are times when that fits our lads and while we do not have the technical attributes of the South American players we have other qualities that they envy. We have a strength of character that Latin nations envy and we are a proud nation and that cannot ever be discounted.'

The major problem which troubled both Brown and Miller was having to tell some of the players that they would not be playing in the glamorous opener. Decisions had to be made and Brown, who had the ultimate choice, was not going to shirk from the face-to-face talks with players when they would be told the team. The delay in naming the team was not because he wanted to hold off telling some of the players the bad news they dreaded, it was simply his way of attempting to steal any advantage he could get by leaving Mario Zagallo (and Zico, of course) in the dark. Brown was determined to get any edge he could for his players and while many of us had our own thoughts about the side he would select, it was only after training on the night before the game that Brown broke his silence to hint strongly at the men and the formation which he had decided upon. Before leaving Provence and their hotel haven there, Brown and Miller had gone around all the players in the group, talking to them about the game, hearing their views and generally assessing the way each man was approaching the greatest game in Scotland's history. Only after that did they sit down and choose the 11 men who would begin the game against Brazil, and it was after training before the players were told.

Then, in the Stade de France, Brown announced the team and, later, as the players returned to their hotel in Chantilly, to the north of Paris and close to the suburb of St-Denis where the stadium had been constructed, he spoke to the press corps. Still, though, he kept the team under wraps, away from the foreign journalists at the conference, and chose instead to speak to his own Scottish group and give them the side. The single surprise was that Celtic's Jackie McNamara had been left out in favour of his club-mate Darren Jackson. Other than that the side was as expected, with Brown persisting in his use of Christian Dailly down the left flank.

The 11 asked to face the Brazilians were: Jim Leighton (Aberdeen); Colin Calderwood (Spurs), Colin Hendry (Blackburn Rovers), Tom Boyd (Celtic); Craig Burley (Celtic), Darren Jackson (Celtic), Paul Lambert (Celtic), John Collins (Monaco), Christian Dailly (Derby County); Gordon Durie (Rangers) and Kevin Gallacher (Blackburn Rovers).

There had been hints that Jackson might be used up front with Gallacher, but it had always seemed to me that the partnership which finished the qualifying games with so much success would be restored if Durie was fit – which he was of course. Jackson, though, was required to fulfil another role in the team. While he was wanted in midfield when Scotland lost possession, he was also the man Brown looked to provide an attacking option on the right. Whereas most people saw Robert Carlos as a danger man for the Brazilians, the Scotland manager took another view. He looked at the space which was left behind the full-back when he moved forward and he wanted to exploit that.

Burley, who preferred to play a more central role in midfield, was not given his wish this time round because the manager was looking to his strength to stop Roberto Carlos when he did raid down the left. If Burley stopped him, went the logic of Scotland's coaching staff, then Jackson could take advantage of the gap which had been left and where neither of the Brazilian centre-backs, Aldair or Junior Baiano, particularly liked to operate. It was encouraging to think that Scotland were continuing to take a positive look at the game, that here they were readying themselves to face a television audience of around two billion people and talking matter of factly about the possible troubles they could give Roberto Carlos. This was the stuff dreams are made of. As we fought our way back to the centre of the city through the rush-hour traffic, listening to the sounds of revelry from the bars and cafés where the foot-soldiers of the Tartan Army were gathering, there was a growing hope that Scotland might, just might, be able to get a draw. The fact this was the opening game helped to contribute to that thought, but so, too, did the general attitude of the Scottish squad and the down-to-earth realism of Craig Brown as he studied the huge task ahead but refused to allow the enormity of it all to affect him. At the very least, I reasoned that night, the team would not be disgraced. They would be able to leave the Stade de France without being humiliated, and they would be able to allow the supporters who had travelled to back them some cause for celebration. They would be able to march on Bordeaux and St-Etienne with their heads held still high and their hopes and dreams still intact. Tomorrow we would know.

IV

The Boys from Brazil

Over the years it has seemed that Scotland have perished from, in the phrase used by the late Jock Stein at the World Cup in Spain, self-inflicted wounds. Sometimes these have happened off the field when star players have self-destructed in spectacular fashion. Sometimes it has been on the field when errors – the collision between Willie Miller and Alan Hansen against Russia in Spain, which prompted Stein to use these two words – have sent the team crashing to defeat.

On this occasion, though, with those two billion people around the world watching, Scotland suffered defeat in the cruellest way imaginable after the team had performed even better than the most optimistic of observers could have hoped.

That other phrase 'gallant losers' springs to mind and it's one which has been attached to the national side on too many of these big occasions now. Here, though, it was apt, because against the awesome power of Brazil, Scotland lost to an own goal 18 minutes from the end of a game where they had held their own against the South Americans and won new admirers for their composure and their courage.

But, first, let us go back to the beginning, back to the seemingly endless hours before kick-off as the supporters tramped around the giant modernistic stadium on the ceaseless search for tickets. Even professional footballers joined the Tartan Army – the Hearts captain Gary Locke leading his own little group.

Locke, like the others, was wearing the kilt and as you watched him mingle with the ordinary fans you realised, if you had not done so before, what this game meant. This was the summit for Scotland, the greatest game they had ever been asked to take part in and they did not intend to take a mere walk-on role. Scotland were not there as a supporting act either on or off the field. That morning every *place* in the French capital played host to its own Tartan Army platoon. The fans were everywhere, thousands of them were ticketless but still determined to add their own splash of colour to the celebrations. Being realistic they expected defeat. All they hoped for was a performance which would allow the team to move on to the next game with some degree of confidence. All they wanted was to leave Paris with a glimpse of that second-round place still tantalisingly ahead of them. It was not a lot to ask for. And then when the team came out with their own salute to the fans, wearing full Highland dress, it was as emotional a moment as the Scottish fans will ever enjoy. They swaggered on to the field, kilts swinging, and those of the Tartan Army who had been able to get their hands on these precious tickets rose to acclaim them. It was a moment for so many of the supporters, one which said to them that the players, too, believed in the country with the same fervour that the support demonstrated, time after time, in game after game, in country after country and on continent after continent. The abiding wish was that more of them could have been there, that more of the ordinary supporters had been able to buy tickets for this match. But the powers that be, the tournament organisers and FIFA, had bowed to corporate demands.

Block after block had been sold to the sponsors and the tales afterwards were of genuine fans sitting next to people who knew nothing of the beautiful game. This, you see, was an event. It was a global happening and the movers and the shakers were out in force, while Scotland and Brazil fans stood disconsolately around a giant television screen in the centre of the city ready to watch their teams play their game. It has always been that way, but in Paris it seemed even more so than normal. Yes, the Scots and the Brazilians made some noise from the wedges of support they had gained between the ranks of fat cats. It was not, though, the emotional full-throated support you would normally have expected. It was more polite, more well mannered, more muted than ever it should have been. It was to the credit of the two sets of players that they rose above that, that they soon forgot the pomp and circumstance which preceded the kick-off, that they celebrated the game themselves with the Scots certainly knowing that this was their finest hour.

Craig Brown had promised beforehand that there would be no 'Braveheart exhortations' in the dressing-room or when the teams took the field. This was the time for out-and-out professionalism he had explained and while the kilts had been used as a motivating factor no other gimmicks intruded. Brown wanted a performance from his team that he could look back on with pride, that he could savour in the years to come, and he told the players, too, that they had to make the most of this match because it might be they would never again play in a match that had attracted so much interest from all over the world, nor one which might mean so much to their proud, if tiny, nation.

Within four minutes the dreams that every Scot had clung to since the draw was made six months beforehand, seemed to turn to ashes when Brazil scored a goal which sent them ahead. The samba rhythms beat around the stadium as the stunned Scots sat in their section in dismay and disbelief. This was not how it was meant to be, they seemed to be saying to themselves.

And, of course, it wasn't how it was supposed to be, because the Scottish defence fell to the kind of goal which would have been embarrassing on the training ground, and which was even more so with the world watching!

Rivaldo had taken a corner on the left and when Cesar Sampaio came to meet the ball neither Craig Burley nor John Collins were there to pick him up. He reached the ball, headed it on target and Jim Leighton was beaten and Scotland were sadly, sickeningly, behind to a sucker punch which would not have concerned them normally. Whether it was nerves, which would have been understandable, or whether it was a little bit of carelessness, which could not be excused, we shall never know. What the world did know, however, was that Brazil had gone ahead in the opening minutes and the global belief that the Scots were there only to make up the numbers had a suddenly uncomfortable ring of truth about it. Those of us who had travelled the campaign trail with the team recognised the limitations which were there, but defending against set-pieces had not caused them any worries in the past. Now we wondered if they would be able to find the rhythm they had shown in the United States, if they would be able to settle into the patient build-up which had suited the players so well in the warm-up matches. It was asking a lot from them.

After all, these were the world champions Brazil who had taken the lead. And the players responsible for the near-post muddle had to pick themselves up and shake off any hangover from that unhappy fourth minute. It was then, though, that the strength of character which Alex Miller had talked of came to the fore. Miller had claimed that it was a quality that the Latin countries envied and here came the evidence to support his claims. Scotland's players began to recover and adapt to the possession game that they had worked on so assiduously in the weeks before the finals. It took time and Leighton had saves from Ronaldo and Rivaldo as the Scots tried to piece their game together. Soon it happened and the Scots were starting to find the little weaknesses in the Brazilian defence that they had been told to look for. There might not have been many, but they did exist. That in itself must have been encouraging to the Scots as they set off on the road which they hoped would lead to some kind of recovery before the Brazilians might do more damage to their cause. Nine minutes before half-time they were given the break their play was due, Kevin Gallacher was barged down in the penalty box by the Brazilian goal-scorer Cesar Sampaio and the Spanish referee, José Garcia Aranda, no doubt mindful of the FIFA warning and of the presence in the stadium of the top brass, awarded the penalty and brushed aside the protests of the Brazilian players. It was a challenge which might have been avoided but it was a measure of the manner in which the Scots were carrying the game to the South Americans and harrying them at every opportunity that the midfielder made the error.

We all knew who would take the kick because that had been decided. Only days earlier Brown had delegated responsibility for any penalty kicks awarded to John Collins and now the midfielder stepped forward and sent the ball low and confidently beyond Taffarel and suddenly there was reason for the support to celebrate. Perhaps, after all, there was to be a sea change in Scotland's World Cup luck; perhaps, at last, the second round place would become a reality. Something they could savour, something they could recall in years to come.

For more than half an hour they were able to hold on to that belief – and able to do so with a degree of confidence as Cafu wildly cleared a dangerous low cross from Kevin Gallacher and Taffarel was tested by Craig Burley – who had promised to shoot whenever he was given the opportunity. However, just when it seemed that the Scots were comfortable and that Brazil might now happily settle for a draw, came the killer goal. When it arrived it was a tragedy for the Celtic captain Tom Boyd. By this time

Zagallo held sway on the Brazil bench and first of all he sent on Leonardo and then, with 20 minutes remaining, Denilson took over from Bebeto. When a diagonal ball was struck across field Cafu burst forward to reach it first, beating off a challenge from the back-tracking Durie to do so. Inside the penalty area he shot, Jim Leighton parried the ball and it broke from the keeper and struck Boyd as he came in to assist. Then it spun from the defender, past Leighton and then past the captain, Colin Hendry, who was on the line. The Brazilians could not believe their luck. The Tartan Army did not believe their own, because they had seen this so often before – though never quite as tragically as on this occasion.

There were later opportunities. Gallacher and Durie shot over, Burley had another drive stopped by Taffarel and in the closing minutes John Collins had a free-kick from the edge of the box blocked by the Brazilian defensive wall. Later, television replays showed clearly that Dunga had handled but no one in the stadium would have expected a second penalty to be awarded against the world champions – and it wasn't – and Scotland trudged from the field trying to come to terms with a defeat they had not deserved and knowing that, once again, they faced an uphill struggle to qualify.

It is a moment which Boyd will live with for the rest of his life, but he was blameless. Indeed, if the ball had struck him on the main part of his body it would probably have dropped down short of goal. However, it hit his shoulder and took a wicked bounce past Leighton and on past the despairing Hendry. Just a few inches would have made the difference, but it was not to be. Afterwards Boyd admitted: 'That has to be one of the worst feelings of my life. There was just nothing I could do about it because the ball came back at me so quickly.

'To think we lost such an important game to that goal – it's horrible. And we had played well and had been able to match up to the Brazilians for almost the whole game and we denied Ronaldo the space he wanted. This just seems to be typical of what happens to Scotland when they get to the World Cup finals.'

It was something that Jim Leighton had experienced before and something that Craig Brown, too, had learned the hard way in previous tournaments. That is why the team manager remained philosophical as he faced the world's press and told them: 'I am not going to deny that Brazil were the better side today. Over the 90 minutes they showed some superb touches, but I was disappointed in the manner in which we lost the first goal, that was not typical of our normal play. I believe that the way we came back into the match tells you something of the spirit which exists in the side. Other teams going behind to the champions of the world after just a few minutes would have crumbled, they would have fallen apart, we did not do that. We got back to our passing game and when we scored from that penalty we deserved to get the equaliser. It would have been a much fairer result if the score had remained at 1–1 because this was not a game we deserved to lose. Now we have to play Norway and we know that we will have to win that game if we are to qualify. We are good enough to do that. I mean it. Brazil are rightly favourites for the group and we always felt we would be fighting it out with the other two countries for the second qualifying position and that is how it is going to be. Things have not changed dramatically because of the result, all that has altered is that we are terribly disappointed that we did not get any breaks in the game and that our World Cup luck went against us yet again. That's hard to take. But we have to pick ourselves up and start all over.'

That night the team flew back to St-Rémy and their hotel, while in Paris it was a night when to be Scottish was to be someone whom even the hard-bitten Parisians felt sympathy for. It appeared that the French had decided *en masse* that Scotland had been unlucky and that was to be a feeling mirrored around the world the following day. All across Europe the newspaper headlines handed Scotland credit for their part in making the opening match a success and the word 'unlucky' was seen in every language.

There was some consolation in all of that for Brown and the players as they rested in their hotel and surveyed their future hopes in the competition. It did not take any expert analysis to realise that Scotland had to win their second game against Norway in Bordeaux – though with the other group game finishing with the Norwegians coming from behind twice to salvage a 2–2 draw with the North African team, an opening remained for either of the three teams. The one dissenting voice in all the praise which was heaped upon the Scottish performance came from the Norwegian coach Egil Olsen who claimed: 'Morocco worried us a great deal and they are a better team than

Scotland. Indeed, I see the Africans taking a point from Brazil and if that happens all we need to do is to win against the Scots. The group remains very open.'

At least that last opinion was one Brown and his players could share. The Scotland coach, less given to extravagant boasts than his counterpart from Oslo, was examining the options carefully. He was also looking at the performances of the individual players in depth and reached the conclusion that his strike force could yet come good. He had a strong belief in the pairing of Durie and Gallacher and in the six days between the opening game and the clash in Bordeaux he continued to talk them up.

The day after the defeat, in fact, he insisted: 'Both Gordon Durie and Kevin Gallacher are at a kind of peak in their play and I am sure that they will score here in the finals. I don't think this team should be written off because of this defeat. We more than held our own against the team who won the trophy four years ago and who are here in France as favourites to repeat that victory, and we are seeded in the European Championship qualifying games.

'You don't become a seed in a major competition unless you have earned that right. These players have done so and I believe that they can still get to the second phase of this competition. It is not going to be easy to do so but we never did imagine that it would be. Even Mario Zagallo told me afterwards how well we had played against his team. He said: "Your team played well and if you continue to play in that manner for the other two games then it is possible that you will qualify." Now that's from a man who has more experience than any other coach here. So, while we lost the game, we can still see some positive signs coming from the defeat. The downside was the way we lost the first goal. When was the last time we lost a goal from a corner-kick? I cannot remember nor can I recall the team defending a set-piece as badly as we did that one. We take that as an insult, to lose a goal that way. It is not characteristic of our play and then the second goal was desperately unlucky and no one can argue with that. Another couple of inches and it would not have hit Tom Boyd's shoulder and it would have been easy to clear and we would have survived. Anyhow, we always thought that the crucial game in the section would be the one in Bordeaux next week and that has not changed because of what occurred in the Stade de France. The players are saddened at the result, but lifted by the fact that for long spells in the game they were able to hold possession and then give the Brazilians problems. Also, we take heart from the way we handled Ronaldo. He was limited in the number of shots he had at goal, and you are talking here of the man who is looked on as the number-one striker in the world. So there are good things to think about as we prepare for Bordeaux. It's not all gloom.'

V
Awaiting the Egil

Of course, as Brown maintained, the scenario for Scotland was not entirely grim as they started to focus on the next game, against Egil Olsen's Norway, the shock team in Europe over the past five seasons and conquerors of Brazil in a friendly in Oslo just a year earlier. In the town of St-Rémy the locals continued to give their famous footballing visitors their support. Still the team were being told how unlucky they had been and how in the next games things would alter and the Scots would get the result their intelligent approach to the game warranted.

It was the thoughtful manner in which the Scots had played which had brought them so much admiration. They had been portrayed as a 'very British' team and, possibly, a 'rough team', and suddenly Brown's strategy had changed all these misconceptions after one match. One German colleague admitted to me: 'None of the German journalists could believe that we were watching a Scottish team. The way the players kept the ball, the patience they had, the very accurate passing and the clever running off the ball, this was a European team. Oh, and we saw too that, at last, there is a British international side which plays with the modern-styled defence. The game opened people's eyes. No one expected to see such sophisticated football and it would be justice if you were to defeat Norway who do play in the old-fashioned British way.'

The messages coming into the team hotel were in the same vein. They came from back home, of course, and from the locals. But they came from around the world, too, because no matter the result people had seen something in the team to admire. This was not the Scotland of old, simply pumping long high balls hopefully into the opposing penalty area. This was, on the contrary, a team ready to learn from the developments the game had made in other parts of Europe.

The fact that Brown was able to bring in Paul Lambert strengthened his hand as he refined his strategy on the way to the finals. Lambert had learned well during his spell with Borussia Dortmund in Germany's Bundesliga. There he was asked to sit in front of the central defenders, pick up the deep-lying striker, win the ball and play it out of defence and forward to players such as Andy Moller. He won a European Cup medal with Borussia before returning to Celtic, when Brown drafted him into the team on a permanent basis he slotted in perfectly – exactly as the manager had visualised he would. He soon became one of the more vital cogs in the smooth-running side which no longer resembled the Scotland teams of the past – except for their resilience.

In the hiatus between the first and second games – six long days – the tournament continued around the Scots and it began to take shape. There were results, too, which gave heart to Brown and his squad. Italy needed a late penalty – in 85 minutes – from Roberto Baggio to hold Chile to a 2–2 draw and highly rated Denmark defeated Saudi Arabia by the only goal of the game. It was a tournament, as always, where there were to be shocks and surprises, and Brown's assessment of Scotland's contribution so far was heightened as he looked around the other matches.

The harsh truth of Scotland's own position, however, was never avoided by the manager or his assistant. They knew what was needed. Neither Brown nor Miller were under any illusions, and in case anyone believed they were ready to kid themselves on a little, Miller soon spelled out what was required. It was clear, as he talked, that he recalled the finals in Italy in 1990 when Scotland lost to Costa Rica and only a win against Sweden in their second match hauled them back into contention.

And so, in reflective mood, Miller looked towards the future and declared that only victory in Bordeaux would satisfy the Scotland backroom staff. They were simply not ready to settle for a draw, even though mathematically that might still be enough to take them to the second-stage game, which they still saw as their main target.

Explained Miller: 'What is going to be important for the team is to go into our last game against the Moroccans knowing that our fate is in our own hands. That is the really vital thing at this stage. And, to do that, of course, we require a win over the

Norwegians when we go to Bordeaux. We don't want to go into the last match looking over our shoulders for the other result and it's too much of a guessing game trying to work out how that match, Brazil and Norway, will work out.'

As always theories abounded as to how the matches would be decided. Brazil would win against Morocco and then, having qualified, would take their foot off the pedal against Norway and so the Scandinavians could edge through. Or, of course, Brazil would want to keep a 100 per cent record and, also, they would want revenge over Norway for the defeat in Oslo the previous summer. Or it could be that Morocco would nick something from Brazil and the South Americans would *need* victory in that last game. Every possible combination of results was examined.

The fans ran the gamut from one to the other, and in the Bar du Commerce in the centre of St-Rémy they always had yet another reason why Scotland would be able to march on to Marseille and a possible meeting there with Italy in the last 16. The disappointment had faded a little now and in its place there was a return of the optimism which the travelling fans had brought with them from home. After all, ran their new argument, we scored a goal against Brazil and we were unlucky and we should have won and wha's like us anyway? Miller's realism was the antidote for the fresh outburst of confidence around the town.

'It is not quite the same as it was in Italy eight years ago,' he pointed out, 'because then we lost the opening match when we were expected to win it. I think we all believed that the team would beat Costa Rica – but this time we have lost to Brazil and, while we might have got a point out of the match, it is not such a blow as the defeat in Genoa was. When it came to the next game there, we had to play Sweden and the team had to be lifted from what had been a serious setback. This time they feel they might have taken something from the game and their overall performance was good – and they are right. So we don't have to restore confidence as much as we did at the Italian finals.'

The irony of Scotland, playing a continental-style game against Norway, who had gone back to the very direct POMO (position of maximum opportunity) tactic devised in England and still practised there by some clubs, had not escaped the Aberdeen manager. 'I suppose their style of play seems outmoded nowadays,' he observed. 'But you have to admit that it does suit them and it has brought them more success than they have ever known before.

'They are one of the most highly rated teams in Europe – even in the world – and they have built that reputation with the style of play their coach believes in. The ideal situation for any coach is to be able to employ a tactical set-up which suits the players you have at your disposal. There is no doubt at all that Egil Olsen has done that superbly. However, we have something fairly important going for us in this one. Almost all their players are playing in England and our lads see them there, play against them there and the home-based players watch them on the TV all the time, and so they won't surprise us. You can see that style hurting other countries – they beat Brazil don't forget – but we have lads at the back who can handle all of that. High balls being launched forwards are not going to present unusual problems to our three central defenders, are they?'

He was committed to that style of play, and while it had been derided by his critics he simply pointed to the results he had achieved and asked when Norway had ever done better. Even after the draw with Morocco when he came under fire after twice going behind, he hit back at the sniping by stressing: 'There is no need to change the basic elements of our way of playing. We will want to be more careful in our defence than we were in the first game. But other than that what should we change? The tactics are good for the players and they fully support the system which we have been using for the past few years. You do not find players questioning the coach's tactics when results are good, and that is the position we are in at the moment. We will play against Scotland as we always play, by getting the ball forward quickly.'

The outspoken Olsen, who had already angered the Scots by writing them off as the 'worst team in the group', maintained his growing reputation for a lack of diplomacy by suggesting that Mario Zagallo should copy his own approach to the game. Olsen was adamant that Brazil would score more goals and gain more success if they followed the direct route he preached. Zagallo, with enough problems within his own camp, was less than impressed.

The idea did not appeal to him, nor did the fact that Olsen had decided to offer his views on the work of his group rivals. Snapped the Brazilian boss: 'All Olsen does is tell his players to hit high balls into the penalty area. He does not have tactics in the true sense. His team does only the one thing and I do not happen to believe that football should be played that way. He is always talking about Brazil but what he says is of no interest to me. I have more to concern myself with than Olsen's comments.'

Olsen, meanwhile, wandered about his training session wearing his green wellies and then moved into his hotel to study his computer. For it was on that computer that he planned his tactics for each game. As Zagallo commented, they did not seem to change too much, but Olsen had his computer and it was on that machine he hoped to plan Scotland's downfall. What he had not programmed into his beloved laptop, however, was that two of his players would suddenly step out of character – and out of line – and, in a fair impersonation of Scotland stars of old, go nightclubbing a few days before the game against the Scots. The incident happened on the Friday night when two of the players broke out of the training camp at the Britanny village of St André-des-Eaux and headed for the resort of La Baule. The players were caught.

Inevitably, the story broke in the Oslo newspapers that Manchester United defender Henning Berg and the Panathanaikos midfielder Eric Mykland had been in a club and had not returned to the team hotel until after five o'clock on Saturday morning. Olsen, a strict disciplinarian, had stormed that the players were no better than 'a couple of gangsters' but then, in a surprising *volte-face*, had relented and allowed them to stay with the squad after they claimed they had not been drinking.

At a press conference Olsen said: 'If the players had been drinking then they would no longer be here with the squad. They would have gone on the first plane back to Oslo. However, there is no evidence that they touched any alcohol and they have both assured me that they were not drinking while they were out. It is not good that they left the hotel in this way and we have spoken to them about that and they know my feelings. But they stay here and they will both be considered for the Scotland game. We have to move on from this. We cannot let it affect our preparations. The whole team held a meeting about this and the players know they were wrong. That is the end of the matter.'

Back in St-Rémy-de-Provence Brown could have been forgiven a quiet chuckle at a scandal hitting the opposition when, so often in the past, it had struck the Scots. But he was reluctant to enter into any detailed discussion of the Norwegian problem, saying only: 'Any coach would be annoyed at this kind of thing happening during a major tournament, but I don't want to think too much about it. We have our own work to concentrate upon. In any case, the two players are staying with the squad and while harmony can be upset by something like this, that is not always the case.

'The paradox is that a group can bond even closer after there has been trouble and after they have been attacked from outside. Remember how England reacted after the Cathay Pacific carry on? It eventually worked in their favour because the players accepted a "collective responsibility" for what had happened, and the same kind of thing can happen here and it probably will because the Norway squad has always been the kind of unit which is more important than the individual players. That is the way Egil Olsen has worked in his years in charge and it will pay off for him now. From what I can gather, he has closed the door on the matter and when he does that then they will all pull in the same direction. It might even make our job harder when we get to Bordeaux for the game there!'

In the meantime the support from home had raised the spirit of Tom Boyd, as he sought to put the own goal behind him and look to the next game and to possible qualification. Messages by fax and by telephone had been arriving at the team hotel and all of them had been encouraging to the Celtic captain. He admitted: 'I don't want this to sound corny but it has meant an awful lot to me that so many people have taken time out of their own lives to think about me and how I might be feeling. I have been surprised at the reaction and touched by it too. Anyhow, it is in the past and we have to think about Norway and I just hope that the game in Bordeaux will have a little more passion about it than the opener did. There was a tremendous atmosphere, of course, because it was the opening game, but I would have been happier if there had been 20,000 of our fans and 20,000 Brazil fans at the game instead of so many who didn't seem committed.'

The Scottish squad continued to believe in themselves, if not in their luck. And if they required any boost to that self-belief it came from an unexpected source, from within the Norway camp itself. The Liverpool midfield player Oyvind Leonhardsen cast his mind back to the UEFA Cup tie the Anfield side had played against Celtic in the season just past. The English Premiership team had won the tie – but the Norwegian was honest enough to admit that his team had been fortunate to push through to the next round of the European tournament on away goals. At the Hotel Fleur de Lys in La Baule he grimaced as he remembered: 'I was injured when the games with Celtic took place, but I saw how lucky we were to win the tie. It took a very special goal from Steve McManaman at Celtic Park to give us a scoring draw in that game and then they drew – at Anfield. Celtic went on to win their own championship and they have eight players here in the Scotland squad, so we know that there is a lot of quality going to be lined up against us in Bordeaux. This will be the key game in the group for us and for Scotland, I know that this will be difficult and we cannot afford the slightest bit of complacency as we go into the match. If any of our players underestimate the opposition, then we could suffer. For me the game is going to be very finely balanced, more than any of the others in the group.'

The Liverpool man was not the only Norwegian to ignore the views of his coach, Egil Olsen, who had happily written off Craig Brown's team. Bad boy Henning Berg had played with Colin Hendry and Kevin Gallacher at Blackburn Rovers before his transfer to Old Trafford and he insisted: 'Colin and Kevin are world class. I know that from the time I spent with them at Ewood Park. Colin is a magnificent defender as well as being the type of player who is an inspiration to others round about him. Kevin is just so fast that he brings a threat with him whenever he moves on to the ball. In my book either of these two players would be in any of the squads here in France. They could play for any of the 32 countries without having a problem.'

The tributes were encouraging but, essentially, Scotland knew that no matter how many compliments were being paid to them – and there were many – it was going to be down to their performance on the field whether they would be able to keep alive their hopes of qualification. And certainly they could use a change of luck. The dreadful run the country had suffered in various appearances in countless finals had continued with that Tom Boyd own goal in the Stade de France. Surely, one felt, there had to be one occasion at the finals when the gods smiled upon the Scots. If it happened in Bordeaux then the Tartan Army would be booking ahead for the Stade Vélodrome in Marseille and the last-16 position they cherished, but which always seemed to be just out of reach no matter how well the team played, no matter how many times they seemed to deserve a better result than the one they had achieved.

It seemed that there had been no justice and it seemed to many who were in France that this was the year when things would change. Even Craig Brown said: 'We surely deserve to have things go our way once. Just once, that's all we are looking for. That would be enough, maybe, to take us into the next round. We can't go on and on suffering such bad luck, can we?'

VI
And Now the Egil Is Landing

If any one man seemed set on stealing the headlines in Group A – the qualifying group in which Scotland competed in France – then it was Egil Olsen (who – it emerged during the tournament – was a target for Celtic, whose previous coach Wim Jansen had left at the end of the season). The little university lecturer with the penchant for computerised soccer had upset Mario Zagallo, the Brazil coach, with his comments on the tactical approach of the team who were defending the trophy they had won in the United States in 1994.

Now, as the game against Scotland loomed, it was Craig Brown and his team who became the target for his caustic remarks. And his views were as unwelcome at the Scots' hotel as they had been in the Brazilian camp. The probability was, of course, that Olsen was out to upset his opponents as much as possible and by doing so hope that his team would gain some kind of psychological advantage in the remaining games. Certainly, his disparaging remarks did upset the Scottish players. Midfielder Craig Burley, heedless of the rumours that Olsen might be his next club boss, was one of those who responded angrily to the Olsen insults. The Norwegian had described Scotland as 'the poorest team in the qualifying group and not a team which will worry us in Bordeaux'. A clearly furious Burley snapped: 'You have to wonder just what this man is talking about. I just don't understand how he can say something like that about Scotland after the display we put up against the Brazilians. We gave them a little bit of a scare.

'I think you could see from their reaction after the opening game that there was a sense of relief that they had managed to get the three points. I thought we played well in Paris, but more importantly, so many neutrals felt that we had played well and that we had deserved a draw from the game, then he comes along with this kind of talk. It's hard to take, especially when he appears to be in a minority of one. Look, we are professional footballers and if we had played badly against Brazil then we would hold up our hands and accept the criticism. This is different and I don't know why we should sit back and take it. When you look at the way he has his own team playing here in the finals – and any other time you ever watch them in action – they don't try to play football. All they do is hump the ball forward out of defence and try to find the big lads they have up front. There is nothing difficult about that and nothing particularly clever about it.

'We know what they do and we believe that we can handle them okay and then maybe we would be able to shut up their coach for a little while. That is a nice thought. Anyhow, it doesn't matter what he thinks, it's what we are going to do on the field and I don't see them being able to surprise us very much because we know what to expect. Norway are easily the most predictable country at these finals. The style suits them, I suppose, and it creates problems for some of the other nations, but I don't see it worrying any of our lads at the back because, basically, they have seen it all before. There is nothing fresh or new.'

There were, however, changes in the Norway team from that which had drawn against Morocco in the first match. Though, giving credit to Craig Brown, he had already intimated that this would happen.

Before leaving St-Rémy Brown had claimed to know the team Olsen would use in the game in Bordeaux, and when the Norwegian coach named it at eight o'clock in the Stade Lescure in Bordeaux 24 hours ahead of the kick-off, the Scottish team manager was just one name out. The Manchester United player Ole Gunnar Solskjaer, who had collected a knock against the North Africans, was missing because of that injury. The others Brown had expected, just as he had anticipated that Olsen would announce his team in a challenge to Brown to do the same. It was a challenge the Scotland manager declined, claiming again that Olsen had handed him an advantage by giving him time to study the individual players Norway would put out on to the field – and work out the general deployment of these men during the match. Nor was he going to require a computer to do that, Brown already had the knowledge, now he had to put that to good use. That was, he insisted at the stadium after the training session, his intention.

With a little dig at Olsen, Brown smiled: 'If this is the right team

– and it is the one I picked apart from Solskjaer – then I think I shall be able to work out the exact formation all right. But this will make no difference at all to my own thoughts about the game. I will be giving Egil Olsen no clues at all beforehand regarding the make-up of my side. The fact that he has given his side does not influence me. That is how he works. I work my way.'

And so he defused the suggestions from Norway that the reason for not naming his team was that he was running scared of the players Olsen had gathered round him from the English Premiership and other corners of Europe, one he had welded into a cohesive, if unimaginative, unit, but one which still held a degree of danger.

That, though, was more apparent against teams without the Scottish capacity for handling the high balls which were *de rigueur* in all of Olsen's planning. Brown knew that, just as he had known the players Olsen would pick, and now he kept his own side secret to gain what little advantage he could before the kick-off. In any event it was his normal way of working, and Brown had attempted to stick by his routine in order to reduce tension among the players. He was not to be jolted out of that by any of Olsen's ploys. And so all we were given from the manager were hints about the make-up of the team and the tactics to be used. He had played his own mind games at that final training session – the designated work-out each team was allowed on the actual playing pitch 24 hours before each game.

The Scottish manager said: 'We have worked on various different set-ups in training over the past few days because we know that it is not going to be the same as playing against the Brazilians. So we have various strategies we can use and the lads have been practising. But they didn't show anyone here at training what we might be up to. Instead, we moved people around into different areas to confuse any of the Norwegians who were watching. Just a little bit of misinformation for them, if you like!

'All Egil Olsen's talk about naming his team early because he is confident about facing us doesn't faze me at all. He is doing that because it is what he has always done. Well, I stick by my own routine and he won't be able to say anything which could change me. Knowing his side is going to be a help to me – and while we feel confident enough about the game I think that confidence will increase if we keep our side away from them.

'What we have to ponder is how often they will attempt the

crosses into the box from the flanks, always looking for Tore Andre Flo and then having people coming in to support him and looking for any little crumbs that may come from his very powerful and aggressive aerial challenges. I don't worry about him too much because we do have Colin Hendry there and he can take care of him in the air, but we need someone in there beside him. Whether we play three central defenders or not will depend on how many men they push up. If Tore Andre Flo is on his own, then it's a luxury for us to keep three men back to cover only him.'

And so Brown pondered his options, all the while studying the Norwegian team-list he had been given, and seeming to take some more confidence from it with every glance. Again, despite the obvious pressure, because, after all, defeat meant elimination from the tournament before the third and final game in St-Etienne, the Scotland manager was relaxed but tight-lipped about his final selection. He did not look like a man who was carrying all the worries of the World Cup on his shoulders. Perhaps that was because Brown had looked at his players that night and realised that they were up for this game. Whether because they knew what was at stake, or whether because of Egil Olsen's jibes, or, perhaps because of a combination of the two, there was an air of purpose about them.

That had Brown stating confidently: 'I have never seen the players fitter both physically or mentally. They are all ready for this game. Norway's physical presence won't worry us because we know what we can expect from them and are ready for that. We can match them in strength and we can more than match them in fitness.

'In fact, I watched them in their game against Morocco and they appeared to tire towards the end of the 90 minutes. Well, our lads won't tire. I would stake my reputation on that. If we can get through the first 20 minutes of the game with things finely balanced, then we shall win it. But we want to be in front then because we want to win this game.'

These were the words of a confident manager and Brown, for once, had history on his side. The results against Norway over the years had been impressive. Out of the 11 games which had taken place between the two countries, the Scots had been victorious in seven of them, had drawn three and lost just one – with the defeat coming in Bergen 35 years earlier.

Brown, though, is not the type of manager to take refuge in such statistics. He is a realist and that was confirmed when he did name his team before kick-off. He remained loyal to the men who had been impressive – and unlucky – in the opener against the Brazilians. The team was: Leighton (Aberdeen); Calderwood (Spurs), Hendry (Blackburn Rovers), Boyd (Celtic); Burley (Celtic), Jackson (Celtic), Lambert (Celtic), Collins (Monaco), Dailly (Derby County); Durie (Rangers) and Gallacher (Blackburn Rovers).

The temptation to tinker with the team had been there, but Brown had resisted it. He had played safe and stuck by his belief that he had the best defenders to match the giant Norwegian front men The long-ball tactic which Olsen would use did not concern Brown and his players. When the match commenced – with the Scottish fans in full cry behind the team – the manager's game plan looked exactly right for this crucial game.

He maintained the formation that had been used in the first match, but he pushed more men forward and the Scottish players kept possession and patiently passed the ball around the pitch and often made Norway – a team rated much higher than Scotland in the FIFA world rankings – look clumsy and technically inferior. There might have been a penalty awarded when Gordon Durie was brought down, but although the Hungarian referee, Laszlo Vagner, gave the foul he insisted that the offence was outside the penalty box, and there was suddenly a sense of the bad luck that dogged Scotland when they were playing in important World Cup games. When Christian Dailly saw a header cleared off the Norwegian goal-line by Stig Bjoernbye close to half-time, the omens were not looking favourable – even though Scotland were dominating the game. That little piece of luck which Brown looked for, the luck which had deserted his team in the first game in Paris, was still missing. The tactics were right; the team choice had been correct; the style of play was effective against an opposition who, as everyone had known beforehand, were simply prepared to sit back in defence and play long, hopeful balls forward to their strikers; until – less than a minute into the second half – one of those all-too-human errors allowed Norway to score the opening goal. Suddenly the advantage had switched from the smooth-moving, confident-looking Scots to the men from Norway – who had spent the first 45 minutes of the game vainly trying to make some kind of impression on Brown's team. It was a blow.

Indeed, it was the kind of blow, coming when it did, which

would have finished off many teams. Scotland, though, fell back on the team spirit which Brown had fostered throughout the campaign and they recovered from the loss of that goal – which was, sadly, from the coach's point of view, one which might well have been avoided.

In the build-up to the match, Brown had talked of the dangers of diagonal balls played from one side of the field to the other, it was just such a ball which caught out the Scotland defence. Midfielder Vidar Riseth struck the ball in from the left and Havard Flo eluded Christian Dailly to head the ball past Jim Leighton. Flo should have been picked up, but the mistake had been made and Scotland had to haul themselves back into the match if the qualifying dream was to live on.

It is to Scotland's credit that they did so, once again pushing their opponents back into defence and threatening almost constantly as the game wore on. Colin Calderwood went off with an injury – which finished his interest in the tournament – and David Weir of Hearts took over from him, Jackie McNamara replaced his Parkhead team-mate Darren Jackson, but it was the man from Tynecastle who helped his country get the breakthrough they required – and one they deserved. Weir had been on the field only a few minutes when he broke forward out of defence and struck a ball through and into the path of Craig Burley. It was the kind of pass which Brown had always believed would beat the flat back four the Norwegians played, and it did. Craig Burley went between two defenders and then strode forward and lobbed the ball carefully over Frode Grodas as the keeper advanced from his line. The ball dropped into the goal as the roars of relief rang out.

Now the Scots searched for the winner, and the victory which would place them in charge of their own destiny in the competition. There were flurries around the Norway goal, there was pressure placed on the Norwegian defence as their players tired – as Brown had forecast – but the goal which would have meant so much did not come. Instead, Scotland had to settle for the draw and they realised that only a victory against Morocco could give them a place in the second round at the finals. Brazil had beaten the North Africans by 3–0 and so the champions had qualified, if Norway, however, could repeat their victory against Zagallo's team, then they would qualify with them. The chance was there, but not in the way the Scots had wanted it to be. Norway, on the other hand, recognised that of all the three nations challenging for the second spot in the group, the result suited them best.

Egil Olsen did not need his computer to work that out, either. Immediately after the game, the Norwegian coach stressed the point when he said: 'Although we must face Brazil in the last game, we know that if we can win the game then we go through to the second stage. We can ensure that by our own efforts. There is no need for us to rely on anyone else. That is the position we wanted to be in and we have achieved that, although I admit that this was a game which we could have lost. I was disappointed at the performance from my players. The way they started the game was not how we wanted to start. For the first 20 minutes we had a lot of problems, but the goal at the start of the second half helped the team's confidence. We needed that. Then when Scotland scored we lost all our organisation once more.

'It was then, during that closing 20 minutes, that I felt we might not survive. But we did, and now we must prepare ourselves for the Brazil challenge. We defeated them last summer so it is not beyond the players to surprise them again. We shall see.'

Olsen was like a man who had been let out of jail, while his opposite number, Craig Brown, was the man who had found the Fates conspiring against him and his players for the second time in the tournament. Shaking his head in disbelief, he admitted: 'We are desperately disappointed that we did not win the game. We should have won it. Anyone watching the game would surely have to agree with that! They were in charge of the game for only 20 minutes or so after half-time when they were lifted by the goal they scored and we were, naturally, down a little bit.

'It's amazing how often we go behind in games and then have to fight our way back into them. To the players' credit they did that again here, but we do make life hard for ourselves when we should not be doing so. The strength of character in the squad is tremendous. It's unbelievable to be sitting here in Bordeaux tonight with just one point to show for all the pressure we have endured in the two matches so far. And we have not had one little bit of luck at all. What I would like to see is the team going in front against Morocco and then showing just how well they can play. I was happy with them tonight, just sorry that they did not get the three points that they deserved for the manner in which they played and the way they dominated so much of the game. No one else at these finals will subdue the Norwegians as well as we did. You can take my word for that. They did not enjoy those 90 minutes, and yet, while we outplayed them, they end up better off than us.

'They can qualify under their own steam while we have to wait for the result of their match – even if we win against the Moroccans. We wanted to win because we wanted to be in their position in the group, but it has not worked out for us.'

Brown, though, did not attempt to disguise his anger at the way the goal had been lost. He had been upset at the Brazilian goals in the opening game and in his post-match analysis of the Norway game he said ruefully: 'We had been so much in command in the first half that we asked the wing-backs to push further forward at the restart. We felt that we could damage the Norwegians if Craig Burley and Christian Dailly went that ten to 15 yards further upfield. So, when the ball came across, Christian had gone forward and so we had the problem of Havard Flo coming in on the ball to make the header. We were slack, there is no denying that, and we have not been happy with any of the three goals we have given away at these finals. They were not typical of our play and so that is something we have to look at closely before the next match. Look, Morocco will not be an easy job for us. Everyone in the camp is upset that we have not yet been able to record a victory. But the lads know within themselves that they have not played badly. Our two performances should have brought us more than just one point. The other result was okay for us because it may damage the Moroccans' morale a little bit having lost 3–0 to Brazil. Incidentally, I did say that Ronaldo would get goals and he scored in that match and I just hope he keeps on doing that when he goes in against Norway. Brazil will still want to win, even though they have already qualified. I don't have any fears on that score. They did not enjoy losing to Norway last summer in that friendly, that annoyed them, and the number of times the Norwegians have talked about the win hasn't endeared them to Zagallo. I would think that suggestions that Brazil will take the game lightly are way off the mark. They won't do that, I know they won't.'

Brown did, though, recognise that there was always a strong possibility of a repeat Norway win because the South American defenders did not relish the direct play they would be asked to counter. While Scotland found few problems with the Norwegian tactics, there was little doubt that South American countries found it difficult to handle. They did not like the aerial bombardment and they did not enjoy the physical threat that the towering Norwegian strikers brought with them on to the field.

That, though, was for Mario Zagallo to worry about. Scotland had their own concerns, even though Morocco had lost so emphatically to the world champions, there was no doubting their talent. When the draw had been made in Marseille back in December, most observers there had described them as the 'best of all the African teams' who would take part in the finals. That was warning enough for anyone and, of course, Brown would be forced into making changes to his team. Colin Calderwood had been flown back to London after an X-ray in Bordeaux had shown he had broken two bones in his hand during the Norway game and an operation was required. He was flown home and although he returned a few days later, there would be no chance of him playing in the third group match, that was always going to be beyond him. Darren Jackson, cautioned twice, was out of the game in St-Etienne as two yellow cards brought an automatic one-game ban.

VII
Morocco and the French Connection

Until the match with Norway was over, the final group opponents who now awaited Scotland had been largely ignored by all of us in the press corps. The hype surrounding Brazil and the opening fixture had been overwhelming and then there had been the belief that the game in Bordeaux against the Norwegians would hold the key to qualification. Now, however, the spotlight was switched to the North Africans who had made their headquarters not far from the Scotland team – just 50 miles or so south, they were to be found in a secluded hotel on the outskirts of Aix-en-Provence and it was there that their French coach, Henri Michel, held court when the countdown to the final, critical group game started.

While Morocco had not yet impinged on the thoughts of those outside the squad, Craig Brown had already watched them, and one of his coaching staff, Frank Coulston, had seen them in a friendly against Chile in Avignon, as well as taking in the group games they had been involved in. He had identified danger in the skills of Mustafa Hadji and Bassir – who both played for Deportivo La Coruna in Spain – and had also warned that the Africans were technically good and well organised. The partnership between the two attacking players was important to the Moroccans, who relied heavily on the understanding the two had at both club and international level, with Hadji causing problems for defenders by dropping off the front men and playing in what coaches term 'the hole' – that vital area just off the front men.

They had drawn their friendly, gone on to draw once more against the Norwegians – when they had refused to be intimidated by the power-play of the Scandinavians – and, surprisingly, lost by three goals to Brazil. That result gave Scotland heart, but Hadji was upbeat after the defeat in Nantes, claiming: 'While we were disapponted with the result and in the way we played – this was not our best form – we realise that we were playing against the tournament favourites and against a team we shall use as a model for our own efforts. Scotland cannot compare to the Brazilians as far as individual stars are concerned, although their teamwork in the two games they have played has been impressive. But we shall be ready for the Scots. That is all we shall think of now.'

The Norwegian camp, meantime, continued their little mind games with giant front man Tore Andre Flo insisting: 'Scotland surprised us. They were the better team and I think that they will be too good for Morocco. I know that I would rather be playing the Africans in our last match rather than Brazil. I don't like to say it, but Scotland are favourites for second place. I thought our goal would have finished them, but it didn't, and they ended the game stronger and better than we did. It was not easy to create chances against them.'

At the Moroccan team's hotel there appeared to be more good news for Craig Brown and his men, as Henri Michel revealed his worries over the goalkeeper he had brought in for the finals and who had now lost five goals in his two appearances. The Frenchman looked relaxed, but whenever the talk turned to the goalkeeping position it was clear that he was under fire from his adopted country's press for his pre-tournament decision which saw him favour Driss Benzerki over Abdelkaber El Brazi, who had been first-choice keeper throughout the qualifying campaign and then on into the African Nations Championships, which had been played some months before the World Cup finals. Michel defended Benzerki against the criticisms which surfaced frequently during his press conference and he snapped: 'I have had problems with goalkeepers since I took over this job in 1995. It has always been there and nothing has really changed. When we came here to France I believed in Benzerki. I thought he was the man who looked in the best condition and, therefore, I selected him. Now he has made mistakes, I admit that, and he has been punished for them, but there is very little more I can do for him because I am only a football coach and his problems right now are nothing to do with his ability or with his physical make-up. If that was the case then I could work with him to help eliminate the problems. But he is suffering from a lack of confidence right now, and if I continue to tell him that he is making errors then his confidence will drop lower and lower. I still believe in his ability as a goalkeeper but his psychological condition at this moment is worrying. A goalkeeper without confidence does not help any team and that is the situation we have in the squad now. One goalkeeper is unhappy at being out and the one who is in the team is conscious that he has made mistakes in the two matches. Against Brazil it was not all the fault of Benzerki, although there were goalkeeping mistakes. We had players making mistakes in other areas of the pitch simply because they were overawed at facing Brazil. They just could not handle the situation they found themselves in and we suffered.

'Too many of my players did not have the belief that they should be there on the same field as the world champions. It was not just the goalkeeper who brought about the loss. It was the fact that too many of the players froze on the night in Nantes and, again, there was nothing I could do about this as a coach. I had talked to them beforehand about the Brazilians and tried to impress on my players that they had to match them, but I could not convince them at all. Sometimes that happens – but it won't happen against the Scots. We know they are a good solid team but they are not Brazil, and so my players will be back to the form which brought them here to France out of the qualifying group.'

Scotland were making much of their ability to outlast their opponents and, certainly, against Norway that had been an important factor as they equalised in the second half and came close to snatching the winner that their play deserved. The backroom staff reckoned that this could be important against the Moroccans if the heatwave which had struck France continued, even though St-Etienne lay slightly further north and the game was to be played in the evening the temperatures would be higher than normal for the Scotland players while perfectly suitable for the Africans. The wisdom of following the training-in-the-heat programme laid out by the medical staff had paid off so far. Now it had to work again and the great thing about the decision was how it was accepted by the players. They knew it had worked for them before and they knew, now, that it was working again. An astonished Gordon Durie, following the game in Bordeaux, had said of the Norwegians: 'They were dropping like flies in that second half . . .'

And the goal-scorer for Scotland, Craig Burley, added tellingly:

'After an hour or so of the game they were done.' That was when the temperature finally struck the Scandinavians and yet the Scots did not suffer any kind of obvious reaction. Yes, there was weight loss, but they knew to expect that. The games in the United States – especially in the searing heat of Washington – and then training in similar conditions in Provence, had given the players a resilience which had stood them in good stead over the first two games. One of the most important factors was that because of the preparations none of the players had to be asked to modify their normal approach to the games. If the heat had affected them, then some of the midfielders, who relied on aggressive running, might have to alter their styles. And the front players, Kevin Gallacher and Gordon Durie, might have had to limit their runs in behind defenders to ensure that they lasted the full 90 minutes without their performance being diminished. Psychologically, it had been important to the Scotland squad that they had been able to outlast their earlier opponents, because they were all aware that in the conditions current in France any advantage was passed to the Moroccan players. Knowing that that would not be the case, gave the players an added reason to believe that the second-phase game was not yet out of reach.

Even suggestions which began to percolate from Egil Olsen's press conferences – yes, him again – could not disturb the Scotland preparations. It was being said that Brazil would not be trying too hard in their last match, which would allow Norway the victory they required to take second spot and Scotland and Morocco would be taken out of the equation no matter what.

Craig Brown's right-hand man, Alex Miller, was particularly scathing over the forecasts being made by the Norwegians. As the Scotland assistant coach pointed out, Olsen had been disparaging in his remarks on Brazil's style and on Zagallo's tactics, and had done nothing to endear himself to the world champions.

As well as that, Miller emphasised: 'What the Norway coach said about Scotland before our match in Bordeaux angered the players. It fired them up for that game and I am sure that the Brazilian lads will have a similar reaction after what he has said about them. Also, they did not enjoy losing last summer in Oslo and have certainly not enjoyed having that result brought up time and again by the Norwegians. Whatever he has said is likely to backfire on him and, if you think about it, why should Brazil simply lie down in a game? What would be the sense of that? They are here trying to win the

World Cup again, and to do that you have to get a team to improve steadily as the tournament progresses. In any case, I think we proved that Olsen was wrong in his assessment of us, and I believe that he will be just as far off the mark in the forecasts he is making now.'

The noises emanating from Nantes were an interruption that the Scots did not need as they stood, in Miller's memorable phrase, 'in the doorway to history'. And soon Brown and Miller began to concentrate on the game ahead, though Miller did concede: 'If we don't qualify then it might be because of what happens in the other game and we know that. After all, we can remember what happened at Euro '96 when we were within seven minutes of getting into the quarter-finals and then a minute later we were out because of what went on at Wembley between England and Holland.

'There was nothing we could do then, and there would be nothing we can do here in France – but what we must try to do is win the game and give ourselves the opportunity of moving a step further in the competition. But these tournaments are very high-pressure events and the fact that most of the squad learned that at the European Championships in England has been of benefit to us here. That was a springboard for what has happened to the team in France. We are now studying the reports we have on Morocco and looking at the video tapes of their games and then we shall talk to the players about them – about the tactics they employ; about how they might deploy their resources; and about the individual players and their strengths and, hopefully, their weaknesses.'

The major weakness, of course, was in the goalkeeping position which had been identified by Henri Michel and which was the subject of some comment from Frank Coulston, the SFA coach who had been handed the task of collating most of the information available on the North Africans. He had fully expected the initial first-team choice, El Brazi, to be used.

Looking slightly bewildered by the turn of events, Coulston admitted: 'I was really surprised when Benzekri was in goal when the tournament started. When I watched them earlier in a tournament that they held in their own country just before the finals, it was El Brazi who was in. He was still there when they played a friendly warm-up game against Chile in Avignon and when he did not appear against Norway and Brazil I thought he must be

TOP: Scotland captain Colin Hendry leads the players in training. He is flanked by (*left*) Colin Calderwood and (*right*) Tom Boyd

ABOVE: Colin Hendry puts pressure on Rivaldo during the opening game of the World Cup finals

RIGHT: Ronaldo and Tom Boyd seem determined to swap shirts before the end of the match

ABOVE: Colin Hendry and Craig Burley fend off the aerial challenge from Cesar Sampaio, Bebeto and Rivaldo

RIGHT: Colin Hendry, this time in an attacking role, is crowded out by Aldair and Junior Baiano

ABOVE: Christian Dailly takes the ball past a Norwegian defender as Scotland try to get the winning goal

LEFT: Norwegian striker Tore Andre Flo endeavours to shield the ball from Colin Calderwood

ABOVE: Watched by team-mates Colin Hendry and Craig Burley, Paul Lambert clears a Moroccan attack

LEFT: A disconsolate John Collins salutes the Tartan Army after Scotland's 3–0 defeat against Morocco

RIGHT: Moroccan goalkeeper Benzekri beats Scott Booth to the ball during Scotland's final group game

ABOVE: It's only a pylon,
the Eiffel's only a pylon

RIGHT AND BELOW: The Tartan Army's
footsoldiers begin their march

Two faces (at least) of the Scottish
support. (Thanks to Susan Spalding for
photograph)

OPPOSITE PAGE
TOP: The desperate search for a ticket
CENTRE: Wullie and his canine-
seeking crew
BOTTOM: A rare photograph of Scots not
lifting their kilts

ABOVE: Spot the fan who is having a good time

LEFT: Tom Shields and Ian Black find an appropriate street in Toulouse for their publisher's French offices. (Thanks to Melanie Stewart for photographs)

LEFT: Ian from Perth swaps tops with Alison from Nashville, USA
RIGHT: Two beers for a tenner meant that during the World Cup the Scots boosted the French economy by about a million quid

injured, then we discovered that, in fact, he had been dropped and the other fellow had been brought in as a replacement. To be honest, I felt that El Brazi was the better of the two but he is now out.

'There is no doubt that Benzekri's confidence has been affected by losing five goals and it will be interesting to see what Michel does now. We have seen weaknesses in the goalkeeping position but in this game you just never know, he may come out and play a blinder against us. It's their problem and they will be dealing with it and we might be better saying nothing.'

Michel, the chain-smoking Frenchman, was meanwhile trying to take any steam out of the meeting with Scotland. When the draw was made he had been reported as being critical of the physical approach he expected from Scotland. Now, after the evidence of the first two games, he had taken a different stance. While denying the original remarks, he was heaping praise on the new-look Scotland.

'On the field in the tournament so far, Scotland have played with great discipline and organisation,' he commented. 'I admire them for the way they have been able to impose their style of play on the opposition, especially against Norway. That has handed them the initiative and we must attempt to stop them doing the same thing to us. We have to assert ourselves but that will be difficult because the Scottish players have a strong commitment and they are very fit and physical. But that does not mean they are rough. I may have been reported as saying that but it is not true; I never said it. Never! It is not true, as the Scottish team have demonstrated in the games against Brazil and Norway. They are strong and they can be physical, but they are also very fair.'

The statistics from the game in Bordeaux, of course, supported the fresh views of Michel and justified Brown's own stance when the barbed comments were first reported. It was always Brown's view that the proof would be out there on the field of play.

And in the Stade Lescure against Norway, arguably the team at the finals with the most physical presence, the Scotland players had just five fouls awarded against them in a game which carried such massive importance. It was to the credit of Brown and his coaching staff that they had instilled discipline, as well as patience and tactical awareness, into the squad as they prepared for the matches at the finals. It was a notable achievement and one which impressed many of the neutral observers. The days when the Scots were looked down upon as a team of cloggers who would hit long, hopeful, high balls into the opposition penalty-box, rather than try the patient build-up so beloved of the European and South American nations were long gone. Some lessons had been learned at last and not the least of those was the defensive set-up, Brown had opted for the three-at-the-back strategy which had been more or less shunned by British teams despite it being the favoured set-up of much of the rest of the world.

It was to be a problem that the trio who Brown relied on so much would be broken up for the match against Morocco. Colin Calderwood had returned from London and his operation, but he was not going to be ready to play in the third game alongside his long-time partners, Colin Hendry and Tom Boyd. The solid base upon which much of the team's success had been built was being disturbed, and that was going to prove crucial. Brown's success in qualifying for two major tournaments back to back had come about by a consistency on selection, as well as a consistency in tactics. Once he had settled on his formation and the players he would have as first choice there had been some tinkering here and there but no major changes and now, as this crucial game loomed, some had to be made.

They were not massive but, nonetheless, Brown was having to face up to the fact that there were alterations which would be forced upon him. He had no control over this, just as he could not control the events which would take place in Marseille at the same time as Scotland went into action a few hundred miles north in St-Etienne. He had hoped to avoid disruption, but the reality of tournaments such as the World Cup is that suspensions and injuries are always going to happen and that no team is immune from change. What did happen this time, however, was that Brown broke his normal habit of keeping his team under wraps until just before the game, he announced the starting 11 shortly after he had supervised the training session at the Geoffrey Guichard Stadium, 24 hours before kick-off. Brown had decided that David Weir of Hearts would replace Calderwood, that Jackie McNamara would replace his suspended team-mate Darren Jackson, which would allow Craig Burley, another Celtic star in this equation, to take the more central midfield role he desired and preferred. There had been a chance that Blackburn's Billy McKinlay would force his way into the midfield but he, too, was injured. And, again, he was sent home to see a specialist about a recurring injury, which had meant he would not be able to play in the finals even if Scotland did qualify.

The team, therefore, was to be: Leighton (Aberdeen); Weir (Hearts), Hendry (Blackburn Rovers), Boyd (Celtic); McNamara (Celtic), Burley (Celtic), Lambert (Celtic), Collins (Monaco), Dailly (Derby County); Durie (Rangers) and Gallacher (Blackburn Rovers).

These, then, were the men entrusted with the task of making history, with taking Scotland into the second stage of the finals.

VIII
History Proves Too Elusive

In a contrast to the normal approach to games, Craig Brown had declared his hand while Henri Michel, in a press conference performance complete with Gallic shrugs, refused to move from his usual routine. He was not concerned that Scotland had named the 11 players they would rely upon, like Brown had waited against Mario Zagallo and Egil Olsen, it was now Michel who delayed, looking for any advantage which might accrue from that.

He did, admittedly, have injuries, and he stressed: 'Until I look at the players again in the morning I cannot make up my mind. I know the team I want to play, but I must run fitness checks on some of the players before I announce the selection. This is too important a game for me to start to take chances.'

Then he added: 'I think that the Scots are a naturally confident race but, while their performances have been impressive here in France, their results have not been very good. There is no reason that they should come into a game against Morocco feeling overconfident. We know that we shall have to attack if we are to win this game. Our biggest mistake would be to let the Scots dictate the pace of the game and the direction of the play. They were successful in doing that against Norway and we shall not be falling into the same trap as the Norwegians in this game. We believe that we can qualify and we shall be aiming for that second place in the group. It is what the country demands from us. We cannot let people down the way we did against Brazil.'

Of course, Michel and the Moroccans were not alone in recognising the expectations of the people left at home. Craig Brown was conscious of that, conscious, too, that the historic aspect of the game for Scotland – the players were desperate to be the first to qualify for the second phase – was an added psychological burden. No matter the experience the team had gathered over the past few years, this was something that only veteran keeper Jim Leighton had experienced before.

Because of that, Brown's plan was to ease any pressure the players might be feeling as the hours ticked away.

'I don't see that there is a need for any rallying call for this one,' he grinned. 'My gut feeling here is that the main job for myself and Alex Miller, and the rest of the backroom staff, is to calm the lads down, all of them are very well aware that they are within 90 minutes of making history for themselves and their country and that is a major situation for all of them to handle. The last thing we need is some kind of Braveheart approach. We don't want that. What we are after is a steely determination and I believe that we will get that in abundance from these lads. They have shown in the past that they are capable of providing that. Now we want it again. I just want them totally focused on the game, not on what is happening elsewhere or what might happen if they win. Just total concentration on the job over the 90 minutes and then when it's over we can assess what has happened. The players cannot allow themselves to be distracted because, if they are, then that is when they might slip up, at this level when you make a mistake then it can mean the difference between victory and defeat. We cannot relax at all.

'What I would like to see happen, though, is for us to go in front. Let's just see what we could do if we had the lead for a change. We have spent the two games here fighting back, and we had to do that against Colombia in New York as well. Just this once it would be a great boost if we were to get the first goal, and the earlier the better. I'll be asking the players to retaliate first in this one and then let the opposition come and try to get the goal back. Ideally that would be the answer for us, that and a display similar to the one we gave against Switzerland at Villa Park in the last group game at Euro '96. We were in the same situation then because we knew that we had to win that game, and we went out and did so. Then we didn't qualify because Holland snatched a late goal at Wembley – and I suppose the same scenario could be put in place here. But we cannot look at the game in that way. We have to take this game on its own, and when we do that, then we realise that victory is all that counts. If we cannot get a win then we are out. If we can achieve victory then we have a chance of being in there in the second stage of these finals. That is the only thing we can think about during the game. Obviously, I shall stay in touch with what is happening in Marseille but I won't allow it to interfere with the job we have here in St-Etienne. Look, there is nothing we can do about the other game except wait for the result. We cannot influence what happens between Brazil and Norway. What we do have to accept beforehand is that if there is any team in the tournament who can upset Brazil then that team is Norway, because they will play to their strengths and that is something that even the world champions cannot always cope with.'

Norway had already confirmed, of course, that they would continue to take 'Route One' with the Liverpool star Stig Inge Bjornebye stating with all the directness of his team's play: 'We shall have to break down the Brazilian defence with long balls. There is no doubt that they are not happy when they face the kind of aerial power that we have. It was different against Scotland because they can deal with that type of play – though we did get our goal that way – but the South Americans are a little bit on edge when they are asked to counter a high-ball game.'

And so the scene was set and, not surprisingly, when the team was announced before the game began Henri Michel had Benzekri in goal and Hadji, who had been declared as doubtful earlier, was named; meanwhile, it was Scotland who were under strength. And it was Scotland, on that night, who also proved to be under par. The game, the vital game, the game where the team were going to make history, fizzled out into a defeat which also saw Craig Burley, the goal hero against Norway in Bordeaux, red-carded in the second half. And all round the stadium the banners wilted as the Tartan Army realised that this was not to be their night. Any celebrations were placed on hold, because the performance given by the team was more of a prelude to a wake than to a party. But the players kept the worst for last. When Craig Brown had hoped to see them step up another gear, lifting their game that bit more than they had for Norway, it just didn't happen. There is no real explanation as to where it all went wrong – apart from the very obvious fact that, again, the side lost bad goals. Slack defensive play cost them dearly once more, just as it had against Brazil and against Norway.

The counter-attacking play of the Moroccans continually tested the Scottish defence, eating away at their concentration and ultimately bringing goals that, on other, less-fraught occasions, might have been avoided. When the first arrived after just 21 minutes, it was a disaster for the captain Colin Hendry – who was caught out when Bassir eluded him and swept on to place a shot past Jim Leighton. In the previous games, the Scots had fought back, even against Brazil they had equalised and they might well have held the World Cup holders to a draw with a little more luck. In the Norway game, after losing a goal immediately after half-time, they came back to draw and came close to victory.

Again luck did not look their way. There was a hand-ball in the Moroccan penalty box which was ignored, but on this occasion, unlike the others, the Scots did little to earn any luck. Their passing game did not flow with the accuracy or verve that had been evident in the opening two matches. The players, for some reason, looked less confident against the North Africans than they had done against the men from South America. While the Scots made openings before the interval there was little belief in the stands that they were about to stage a comeback. And when the teams went off at half-time the chants and the songs of the Scottish fans were muted. These fans, most of them anyhow, had seen this picture before and it was as if they knew the worse was still to come. It did not take Morocco very long to prove their forebodings correct.

Two minutes into the second half, before Scotland could put into place any of the changes which Craig Brown might have wanted to see implemented following the half-time team talk, a goal was lost. It was down to a defensive error once more, David Weir was involved this time when he failed to stop a through-ball from the Moroccan play-maker Hadji and he had to watch in dismay as Hadda went through and shot. Jim Leighton reached the drive but could only parry it and the ball arched up in the air and dropped over his head and into goal and the game was more or less over. If any optimists among the Scottish support looked for a recovery then even they must have realised when Craig Burley tackled Bassir from behind and was red-carded by the referee from the United Arab Emirates that the dream had died. The ordering-off came seven minutes after the second goal and Scotland were left to play for more than half an hour with only ten men. To be fair to the remaining Scots, they still went forward when they could, as if attempting to salvage some self-respect from the match, as if they wanted to bow out of the tournament still holding on to the reputation they had brought with them into the closing group game. But it was not to be. Five minutes from the end, Bassir struck again, and while the support remained behind to cheer the team, the harsh reality was that on this night of all nights Scotland had not been good enough. On a night when, before the game, there had been talk of history being made, the same sad old ending had been provided. On a night when the Scottish support had begun by taking over the centre of St-Etienne and turning it into a sea of tartan, everything had ended in black despair. Sure, there were parties, but behind the bonhomie was the acceptance that another World Cup had come and gone and another Scotland squad had failed to make the cut. The team which had surprised us so often had run out of surprises at last.

There can be no denying that the team had astounded all of us over the years by qualifying for the European Championships in England, and by qualifying for the World Cup finals in France. And then, too, by the displays they had given in both of these tournaments – until the final game was played and the final act had to be written in the St-Etienne meeting with Morocco. Ironically, of course, even victory would not have carried the team forward into the second phase, they would have suffered as they had in England in 1996 when the late goal for Holland meant they went out. Because Norway, the team who believed they had the Indian sign on Brazil, proved their class in Marseille where they won 2–1. All three goals came late with Bebeto giving Brazil the lead 12 minutes from the end, only to see Tore Andre Flo equalise five minutes later and then Kjetil Rekdal scored the winner with a last-minute penalty after Junior Baiano had handled inside the box. And Olsen later admitted: 'When we heard the score of the other game [Scotland–Morocco] then we had to make changes and we had to take more risks and we did so, and that is what brought us the two late goals and also qualification from the group. Our attitude changed when we heard the Morocco score.'

Now Norway would return to the Stade Velodrome to face Italy, while Scotland returned to St-Remy, disconsolate, to prepare to fly homeward. Probably to think again.

As Brown admitted: 'We just did not play anything like the same way we did in the games against Brazil and Norway. The first two goals we lost were uncharacteristic, and when you get to this level of international football then you cannot afford these lapses of concentration. When you have them then you pay dearly. We found that out tonight – but we had discovered it earlier, too. While our general play in the other matches was much better than it was tonight we still lost goals that we would not normally have given away. That was possibly the most disappointing feature of the three matches.

'As for tonight, it was bad enough to go two goals behind so soon after half-time, but then when we went down to ten men I think we all realised it was all over. We had given ourselves what was virtually an impossible task. The players fought on and they tried to regain some of the pride they had lost, but it was too much for them to do. We have to hold up our hands and say that the better team won the match on the night. What is difficult to accept is that we played so well against the two teams who have qualified for the next-round games and matched them in almost every way, yet here we are going home again. If we had had just a couple of breaks then we would be looking at a game against Italy in Marseille this weekend. It is not really any consolation that Norway beat Brazil because I always felt deep down that that could happen. They are a bit of a jinx team for Zagallo but, as I say, that doesn't matter. What we are thinking about here is the poor quality of our own performance. That is what has to concern me. Of course, while saying that I am not trying to take anything away from the way Morocco played. You cannot forget that they are ranked eleventh in the world by FIFA, and it was always on the cards that they would be able to put on a display like the one they gave tonight. On the night they got their game together – something they were not able to do against Brazil – and we didn't, and yet we did so well against the holders.

'I don't know how you explain that one except to say that they took their chances against us and we were not able to do that, even though we had more shots at goal than they did over the 90 minutes. I did feel some sympathy for Morocco at the end, because if anyone had suggested they would beat us by 3–0 before the game then they would have looked upon that kind of result as a passport to the next stage. Yet, here they are in the same sad situation as ourselves. That is hard for them to take, I would imagine. I know how I would be feeling in their shoes. You have to remember that we have been there. It happened at Euro '96.'

The disappointment of the North African team was soon articulated by their coach Henri Michel who shrugged: 'The players cannot believe what has happened to them. But this is still an important night for African football because we came to St-Etienne as the underdogs in this game. Because of the Scotland matches in the group, and because we had been so bad against Brazil, we were not expected to win. But we have done so and we demonstrated the skills and the ability that exist and flourish in African football. I did not expect Norway to win, and when you have the type of result we enjoyed tonight then you expect to go through. But it was about our pride as a nation, too, and we have regained that after our defeat from the Brazilians. This was truly an outstanding performance from all of the players. It is a game which will live forever in the history of Moroccan football. No other team from this country has ever achieved such an important result as this one has been. We shall cherish it, even in our disappointment at not reaching the second spot in the group which we had aimed for. The result is our consolation prize.'

For Scotland there was little consolation; so much had been expected in that final game; so many dreams had been carried to the town of St-Etienne; so many people both in France and at home had believed that there, for the first time, was a Scotland team who would make the second phase. Yet inside 47 minutes the hopes had been dashed. This was not a disaster on the scale of defeat by Costa Rica in Italy, nor was it approaching the catastrophic draw against Iran in Argentina. The quality of the Moroccan team had always been known – apart from the FIFA rankings it was generally accepted that they were the best team in Africa, where the game is growing in strength as each World Cup comes along. The Scotland backroom staff had not underestimated their last match opponents but, perhaps, most of us in the media had not taken on board the quality which had been attributed to them by so many good judges of the game.

Perhaps their collapse against Brazil and the problems which had been talked up by Henri Michel had given rise to the optimism felt following the way Scotland had handled the first two games – which were played against the world number one team and against another listed at seven. There had been signs in both of these games that Scotland had learned how to play football at this level, and then the roof fell in as it has done so often. Perhaps, as Alex Miller had pointed out earlier in the competition, it is in the Scottish make-up to be more dangerous when you are least expected to win. When any Scottish team is handed the role of being favourite it seems always to sit uneasily with the players, yet write them off and they will fight to prove themselves, but write them up and forget it.

IX

Home Before the Postcards . . .

It was a depressed group of players and officials who arrived at Marseille Airport less than 24 hours after the defeat from Morocco. The previous night, right after the game – as had been the case after the two other group games – Scotland had flown back to their St-Rémy-de-Provence retreat. Then they had held their usual press conference and got down to the business of training and preparation for the next game. Now there was no other game left, nor was there a press meeting organised for the village. Instead, it was staged hurriedly at Marseille Airport as the group attempted to hide their unhappiness at the turn of events which had brought them a second defeat and sent them home with just a single point for their efforts at the finals.

Here they were rushing home as if living up to the cruel jibe which has followed so many Scottish teams to the World Cup: 'home before the postcards'. The special charter aircraft touched down and spirited the players away, while the supporters in France still tried to come to terms with the disastrous result against Morocco. They were not alone in that – many in the official party were similarly affected by a result which so few of those who had been following Scotland's progress towards the finals and in France had expected.

Craig Brown, was as honest and as forthright as always when he proceeded with his post-mortem that afternoon. He, too, had tried to fathom out what went wrong as he sat up into the early hours.

Finally, he explained: 'When we get to this level, the kind of rarified level you find at these very top tournaments, then we just cannot quite hack it. I don't think anyone would argue that we played well against Brazil and Norway, but then at the end we were not able to maintain that level of performance. The top teams can do that. I am not blaming my players here one little bit because we know how hard they worked and prepared for these finals and how gutted they feel now after that one bad result.

'They are all tremendous professionals and it is because of that we have been able to get the understanding and the spirit which has brought us some limited success. Anything we have achieved has come from their readiness to adapt and to blend their skills into the team pattern and make it all a group effort.

'What we don't have is a Ronaldo, or a Zidane, a Laudrup or a Djorkaeff, the type of player who can alter the direction of a game by one piece of brilliance. We are not breeding that type of player at this moment in time. To balance that we have to maximise our resources and fit them into the teamwork which was so vital to us in the first two matches. Then we had a suspension and a couple of injuries to deal with, and when that happened the squad was stretched to its limits. I believe that we do well in qualifying on a fairly regular basis for these major competitions. There are a lot of bigger countries who would happily accept our World Cup qualification record since 1974 until the present time. Take a look at some of the countries who were not here, such as Portugal and Sweden and Russia. Would they have liked being in our position? Of course they would. It is going that little step further which is our problem.

'The strengths we have in our game, the organisation, the ability to retain possession, a strong defence normally, and a tremendous spirit, are good enough to take us to the party. Unhappily, they can't take us to the stage we want to reach so badly. I know the result looks bad and the performance was poor. But it is not the worst than I can recall since taking over as the international team manager. We lost in Gothenburg to Sweden on the way here, and that was a dreadful display. This one is magnified because of what we all expected from the game and that was not only a win, it was also the chance of staying on in France and carving out our own little slice of history. There were defensive mistakes and Colin Hendry has held up his hand for the first goal. He has apologised for being at fault for that one, and we know who was to blame for the other. And after these goals went in we were toiling. I have to say, mind you, that this was probably the one single mistake that Colin made in the entire tournament. Now we have to get home and get back to work and get ourselves ready for the European Championship games which kick off right after the domestic season starts. By then we will have to be making sure that we don't give away the kind of soft, sloppy goals we allowed here. We shall do that and we shall attempt to qualify again for the finals in Holland and Belgium in the year 2000. Despite the disappointment of St-Etienne, there were other good things which came out of the tournament for us. These are what we have to remember when we start off again on another campaign.'

Brown was right. The good and bright and shining memories of the Stade de France and that opening game against Brazil remained.

The goal from John Collins and then the moments in that second half when it seemed that Scotland would be able to draw against the champions of the world.

Then there was Bordeaux, where Norway were played to a standstill and left reeling on the ropes, relieved that they had been able to leave the Stade Lescure with a 1–1 draw which they had not deserved and which eventually contributed to their qualification in second place. Craig Burley's equaliser lit up that night for the supporters and gave the team and the Tartan Army the hope that their ever-present dream could be realised

Maybe some day it will happen, but after watching the gods turn their faces against Scotland in West Germany and Argentina, in Spain and in Mexico, in Italy and then, lastly, in France, I can no longer believe that a Scotland team will ever do anything other than make up the numbers at the greatest football show on earth. There may be moments to savour, moments which lift the nation's hopes, but what Craig Brown said is essentially correct: Scotland is a country which can provide a squad strong enough to battle through to the finals of the World Cup or the European Championships, but is not equipped to then take that success and build on it when the likes of Brazil and Germany and France and Italy come into the reckoning. There is a level our clubs have found in European competition – considerably lower than that of the national team – and when it comes to the big guns of international football we can only make it among the also-rans. Perhaps that will change and there will be a resurgence in home-grown talent and Scotland will have some world-class stars. It would be nice to think so.

In any case, another World Cup adventure was over and this time Scotland left without even a victory, it was the worst performance since they had been in Mexico. There, though, some consolation could be found when you examined the opposition they faced in what even neutral journalists had dubbed the Group of Death. Denmark and Germany and Uruguay were the teams the Scots had to face and even the wiles of Alex Ferguson, who was then stand-in manager of the national side, could not prevail. One point was won there after defeats from both European countries and then a draw with the South Americans.

There were some hard-luck stories to be told, but none which could compare with those from West Germany or Spain, or even Italy. In the end Scotland proved not to be good enough, they were unable to sustain the level of consistency required in such a tournament. In that first game the adrenalin was flowing simply because it was the biggest game any of the players had ever taken part in, and it was still there for the match against Norway, when the players had been angered at the comments made by Egil Olsen who had cruelly written them off. But, by the time they reached that final encounter with Morocco, they had left too much on the previous fields. Perhaps, deep down, they knew that victory had been required against Norway if they were to finish in second place. That had been the target set by Craig Brown and Alex Miller, and one which had been amended after the game had finished 1–1. Then they indicated that a draw could yet be enough, but to some extent they were whistling in the dark. The initiative had been snatched away from Scotland, their destiny was not in their own hands and whenever that occurred the team spirit flagged.

Also, as Craig Burley said before leaving for home: 'Morocco did not let us dictate the game at all. Because they altered their approach we were forced to play more long balls than normal, and that was far from how we wanted to play. But while we are all disappointed at losing in the last game, it was not there that our chance of qualification vanished. That happened earlier. That happened in the first two games when we could take just one point from two matches in which we had played well.

'To be honest, the results apart, we enjoyed the whole occasion. Once you get a taste of this kind of thing then you just want more and I hope that I shall still be in the team if we get to the World Cup finals next time round. I am only 26 so I want that opportunity.

'But, first of all, there is the little matter of the European finals which will be held in Holland and Belgium in two years' time. It would be nice if we could reach three major tournament finals in succession. That has to be the aim. We want to be there and to try to do better at the finals than we have done so far.'

Burley, red-carded in the Morocco game after a reckless tackle which was born out of frustration after Scotland went two goals behind in the second half, became the only Scot ever to be sent off at the World Cup finals. That was a dark contrast for the Celtic man to the celebrations he had sparked in Bordeaux when he scored the equalising goal against the Norwegians. And, in a sense, it mirrored how the finals had gone for the Scotland squad: from tunes of glory to the dirges of despair in the space of a fortnight. That afternoon at Marseille Airport the Stade de France seemed light years away, some distant tartan-clad dream.

Yet the memories remained for so many and the stragglers among the support, some who had optimistically arranged for tickets for the second-phase game at the Stade Vélodrome, where Norway were now going to face the Italians, others who were staying on to watch the rest of the tournament without the gut-wrenching emotion they had been forced to experience while watching Scotland.

They appeared in Marseille, in Paris and at various other venues, forlorn groups still wearing kilts but often, now, with Brazil tops as they switched allegiance to the country whose football the Scottish fans seem to admire more than any other. The Scotland side had gone home, but the support still maintained a presence for the nation, and as roving ambassadors they made certain that no one would ever forget their country's involvement in the 1998 finals.

Defeat had hurt, but it had not been able to eradicate the feeling they had for the game and the pride they could still hold on to after being one of the countries to qualify. As Brown had reminded us all, there were many, many nations who had not been able to qualify, who had been excluded from centre stage, who had not even had the opportunity to take part in the matches and then to return home early.

That was something the Scots who stayed on in France had to console themselves with. The stay had not been long enough, but in its way it had sustained their dreams – until that last tragic act against the men from Morocco. If they wanted to forget that night in St-Etienne none of them wanted to forget the opener against Brazil when Scotland and its footballers were admired around the globe.

X
After the Postcards . . .

After Scotland's departure, the tournament began to take shape as the qualifying groups threw up few shocks. While Scotland's record in the group was a disappointment they were not the worst of the non-qualifiers: Bulgaria, Saudi Arabia, South Korea, the United States of America and Japan were all worse off when goal difference was brought into play.

One of the major surprises, though, had been the failure of Spain in Group D. The team which had been tipped by many as potential winners of the tournament did not come to life until their last game, when they defeated Bulgaria 6–1, but even that stunning result did not save them. They had lost to Nigeria and then drawn with Paraguay, and the Africans and South Americans were the countries to progress.

At the top of the various groups, however, there was that old familiar look: Brazil and Italy, France and Holland, Germany and Argentina, with only Romania and Nigeria unexpected section winners. The giants of world football were, however, in pole position as always, and France – in spite of carrying a heavy responsibility as host nation – had begun to settle, as their group win over Denmark confirmed.

As for the teams who had moved on from Scotland's group, Brazil were asked to meet Chile at the Parc des Princes in Paris, while Norway were in Marseille for their clash with Italy. It was a game where history was on the side of the Italians as Egil Olsen knew.

But the computer coach dismissed all games except those which had been played since he was installed as his country's coach. 'Since that time,' he pointed out, 'we have been able to do well against Italy. Before the European Championship finals in 1992 we won 2–1 in Oslo and drew 1–1 in Genoa and then, of course, they defeated us at the last World Cup in the United States. They scored the only goal of the game then and that prevented us from reaching the second stage of the competition. Now, though, we have gone further than before and we believe that our adventure is not yet over. In any case, the same was said before we played Scotland and that did not affect us at all. We are here and the Scots have gone home and that is the only thing which matters at this level.'

Then he added: 'We know exactly how we want to play and the criticism we sometimes get won't make us change. We have a style which allows us to impose ourselves on the opposition. If we do that against Italy – as we did against Brazil – then we shall win.'

Olsen did appear to be protesting too loudly at the team's Aix-en-Provence hotel after Norway had again been the subject of criticism from one of the other coaches. This time it was the Frenchman, Aime Jacquet, who dismissed Olsen's strategy by saying: 'The gift which the Norwegian team possesses is one which allows them to make their opponents play badly, to haul them down to the same level, and that is not what you hope to see at the World Cup finals. You look for more than that. You look for skill and you look for style, and people want to see the beautiful game.'

Yet, no matter the jibes aimed at the direct play his team used, Olsen was not for turning, and his opposite number, Cesare Maldini, seemed nervous at the prospect of facing their aerial power.

The threat Scotland had been able to largely subdue was still the one which other, more prestigious nations fretted over. The Italians, for instance, were concerned about the heading ability of Tore Andre Flo – the Chelsea front man who had been marked out of the match against Scotland by Colin Hendry. Flo himself referred to that on the eve of the match as he paid a powerful compliment to his departed rivals. 'I know what people say about Italy and how well they can defend in any circumstances,' he declared, 'but this defence will not be harder to play against than the Scotland defence was. It is probably right to say that we did not play well in Bordeaux, but that was down to the approach of the Scots. They simply gave us no room at all and we found it easier to play against Brazil. And now I think we shall find it easier to play against Italy. I do not believe that Italy will be any better organised than Scotland were in that second game. In fact, we have not played any team in the past few years who were better set up strategically than the Scots. They surprised us. It was a game we were lucky to get through without losing all three points. I am happier at the thought of facing Italy tomorrow than I would be at the prospect of playing Scotland again and, yet, our confidence has been so high that we rarely go into games even thinking of defeat. But the Scots were much more disciplined than we ever thought they would be. Still, the good thing is that Italy won't be as strong at the back as Scotland were, and I do think that we shall worry them when we play the ball high into their penalty box. They will be like Brazil – they won't like that – and they will struggle a little to combat our style of play. We are confident about this.'

Cocooned as they were in the self-belief that Olsen had brought to the squad and in the utter certainty that the long-ball tactics were right, the Norwegians were deaf to the criticisms which were hurled their way. The French midfielder and captain, Didier Deschamps, joined in the debate over Olsen's tactics and insisted: 'For the sake of football, for the sake of this great game, then we all have to hope that Italy win the game in the Stade Vélodrome. I admit [the Norwegians] style is effective and it does suit the players they have in the team, but there is nothing to admire there. You can fear what they might do with these high balls but you cannot accept that this is any longer a part of the modern game. They are the one country here in France who play in that way. It is very, very old-fashioned and it is ugly.'

The Italians, though, refrained from being too critical. Instead, they simply admitted that playing against Norway would give them problems and that they would be different from any others they came up against in the competition. Their captain, Paolo Maldini, son of the coach Cesare Maldini, added thoughtfully: 'We believe that we can cope with their attacks and we feel comfortable with the way our form is growing with every game. It is important at the finals to feel that you are improving from the first game through to the others and that is how we are at this moment.'

Craig Brown, returned to Marseille to see the game and he watched as Christian Vieri scored in 18 minutes with a goal which took Italy into a quarter-final meeting with the host nation in the Stade de France. Tore Andre Flo had just one chance and that was held by the Italian keeper Gianluca Pagliuca just after the Italian goal had gone into the net.

Brown said: 'That save was so special it reminded me of the Gordon Banks' stop from Pele in the World Cup in Mexico. It was an incredible save from the Italian keeper, but it has to be said that it was the only time in the 90 minutes that I can recall Flo getting himself clear of his markers. You have to give the Italian coach and his defenders credit for the way they took care of the man they saw as the main threat to them.'

But there was a sense of sadness from Brown, too, a feeling of regret that he was there only as a spectator instead of pitting his wits against Maldini. He admitted: 'It came back to me during the game that a team we had outplayed in Bordeaux – Norway – were out there playing today, while our lads are back home again. It does seem a little bit of an injustice. All through the match today I was thinking how we would have approached things, and I do think we would have posed more questions for the Italians than Norway did. Basically, Norway cannot alter their approach in any major fashion and the Italians knew that and dealt very competently with the problems they knew would be thrown up.'

Norway now left France and the general feeling was that the tournament would see more games of quality now that the long-ball devotees had departed. And the other games suggested that could be the case: Brazil hammered four goals past Chile and Denmark won against the last of the African countries, Nigeria, by the same 4–1 margin. That same weekend France defeated Paraguay 1–0 in an edgy display and two of the quarter-finals were decided – France v Italy and Brazil v Denmark. Soon the others were firmed up, as Germany defeated Mexico 2–1 and Holland won by the same score against Yugoslavia.

Soon Argentina and Croatia were to join them – the Croatians after a single-goal victory over Romania, and the South Americans after an epic struggle against England in St-Etienne at the very stadium where Scotland had gone out of the tournament. A week later, England suffered the same fate and they also had a player sent off when, just two minutes after the interval, David Beckham was red-carded for a petulant kick at Diego Simeone in front of the Danish referee. The teams had been locked at 2–2. Argentina had gone in front after only five minutes with a penalty from Gabriel Batistuta, and then England had fought back with Michael Owen as the main tormentor of the South American defence. First of all Owen was brought down in the box and Alan Shearer levelled the scores with a penalty and then, in the 16th minute, Glenn Hoddle's team were in front when the Liverpool teenager Owen struck with a glorious solo goal. That was cancelled out by Javier Zanetti after he reached a free-kick from Juan Veron and sent the ball past David Seaman before half-time. Then came the Beckham blunder and a valiant defensive display from England, with Tony Adams and Paul Ince immense. They inspired those around them and the ten men held on to force the game into extra-time and then onwards to a penalty decider.

It was then that England failed, then that their nerve finally broke and Argentina were left as victors and given that coveted place in the quarter-finals. Both countries scored with their first kicks and then Seaman saved from Hernan Crespo and Paul Ince followed that with England's second kick, which was stopped by Carlos Roa. Then penalty after penalty was taken and the players scored, until the fifth England kick from David Batty.

Again Roa saved the shot and suddenly England were going home. Afterwards, the former England manager, Bobby Robson, said: 'That is now the third time we have lost in this way, on penalty kicks. The players defended magnificently in the second half but it all ended in heartbreak and in the toughest way possible for the lads to have to accept. Glenn will be devastated.'

The Argentinian coach, Daniel Passarella, captain of the team which won the World Cup in 1978, claimed: 'This is a very big day of joy for Argentina. I was almost in tears when we scored that second goal because everything about it was so perfect. It was a very hard game and England showed tremendous passion when they were reduced to ten men. But we are through and now we have to think of Holland and the game we have against them in Marseille.'

The four quarter-finals were now complete with Holland against Argentina in Marseille and Germany against Croatia in Lyon. Brown still had a hunch that the resilience of Bertie Vogts's men would carry them all the way, but the Scotland manager hedged his bets a little, pointing out that Brazil were still there and that France, despite a little stumble against the Paraguayans when they did not show the form they had done in the group games, were beginning to awaken to the possibility that this was, indeed, to be their year of destiny in the tournament which had been established by a Frenchman, Jules Rimet, but had never been won by the French national side. Gradually, Aime Jacquet was winning over his critics – and they had been many. Poor results in the two years leading up to the finals had been held against him, and the French press had decided that the team's preparations had been poor.

Jacquet had, therefore, been under fire. And even as the French team edged past Paraguay there were those who felt that the national team would not be able to sustain the challenge when they came up against Italy in the Stade de France. But those pessimists were growing fewer and when I returned to Paris after the St-Etienne game – I had been away from the capital since the opening match – I could sense a change in the atmosphere. The public were now beginning to believe that France would win the World Cup, that France would be able to defeat even the mighty Brazilians – the country they would meet in the final if everything worked out as expected, and the results favoured the two countries.

It was the final that the French wanted, the final that the football world wanted, and yet there had been surprises by now and there would be more before the final was played on 12 July.

The first of the quarter-finals to be played was between France and Italy, with a follow-up game a few hours later between Brazil and Denmark in Nantes. The first game at the Stade de France was clearly to be a tactical battle between Jacquet and Maldini. The French coach made that clear as the team prepared for the game, while the Italians tried to heap pressure on to the host nation by talking of the burden of responsibility they were carrying with them in every game they played.

The Chelsea midfield player, Roberto Di Matteo, stressed: 'When you are the host nation at the World Cup finals, or even the European Championships, then it can be very difficult for you. You are expected to win every single game and, to be fair to the French, up to now they have been able to do that. They are the one team left in the tournament which have not dropped even a single point. No one could ask for anything more from their players because they have been able to deliver what their country has wanted, but it is still a problem for them to be at home.'

Jacquet, still hinting at the tactical struggle which was to come, declared: 'There is nothing, absolutely nothing more that I can learn about the Italian team. I believe that this will be the same for Cesare Maldini because he will feel the same about my team and my players. They are all very familiar.'

Many of the players faced each other on a regular basis in Serie

A, and there was always the danger that they would simply cancel each other out on the day, if that was to happen then a moment of genius, a piece of unexpected brilliance, would be necessary to separate them. There were players on the field capable of doing this and one of them, the French play-maker Zinedine Zidane admitted; 'I know all the players from Serie A and they all know me because that is the way of modern football. If you are playing at a high level then your paths must always cross. It was very difficult for me to watch the Paraguay game because I had been suspended, but now I am back to share in this adventure for my country. This is the most important match in my whole career. It is a quarter-final of the World Cup and I have never played in such a game before. But we feel that the nation has united behind us and that is very important for the players.'

It was also the factor which troubled Maldini most, as he worked with his team the day before the match, saying worriedly: 'We want to be in the semi-finals of the tournament, but the threat to us is that France has such a strong emotional need to be there. The supporters will be driving them there and that is a strong force. That is why we are not even talking about the game France played against Paraguay. That does not enter the equation. Perhaps they found it difficult against the South Americans, but they won the game and they are now here, and with every step they take they come closer to what the whole country wants – outright victory.'

The golden goal from Laurent Blanc had given France the win over Paraguay, but there had been a sense of relief when the defender scored – though, as Maldini was suggesting, it had been the one single blip in the games France had played so far.

In Nantes, the Danes made confident noises with Brian Laudrup emphasising: 'We are happy to be facing Brazil. It is better to play against them than some of the other countries who are here in France because you know they will attack. Also there is no pressure on our players at all going into this game. If we lost then people will have expected that – but if we manage to win then it will be the greatest victory Denmark has ever achieved.'

When the games took place they went as most onlookers had expected, a thrilling struggle between Brazil and the Danes and an absorbing tactical struggle between the French and the Italians. That game in Paris went to extra time and then penalties before it was decided – like the England–Argentina game – on the fifth penalty to be taken. Before that, long before that, France should have had the game won, but they missed scoring opportunities and Italy were able to hang on. Then when the penalties arrived, Bixente Lazaruzu saw his kick, the second for France, saved by Pasliuca. Then Fabien Barthez saved from Demetrio Albertini and the nation breathed again.

The Italian midfield player, Luigi Di Biagio, stepped forward to take the fifth kick and as his shot struck the crossbar he dropped backwards on to the turf, while all around him the French players congratulated each other and saluted their fans.

Soon afterwards, in Nantes, the other quarter-final turned into one of the classic games of the competition, matching the England–Argentina game for drama and surpassing it for sublime skills and glorious goals. The game had begun on a high note when Martin Jorgenson scored after 91 seconds when he struck a pass from Brian Laudrup past Taffarel, it was a shock for the champions and one they responded to. In the eleventh minute Bebeto had equalised and then, seven minutes after that, Rivaldo put the South Americans into the lead – both goals had been set up by Ronaldo. Now it was the turn of the Danes to hit back and five minutes into the second half they were able to do so when Roberto Carlos tried a spectacular overhead clearance, he missed the ball and, as he lay helpless on the ground, Brian Laudrup gathered the ball and shot past Taffarel, Brazil were in trouble once more. Still, with just an hour played, the Brazilians underlined that they were not ready to give up the trophy they had won in the United States, Rivaldo was allowed to make ground and then shoot and Peter Schmeichel could not stop the shot and the game was over, and the dream final between the hosts and the holders was still a strong possibility. The match in Nantes had been a classic between two teams with outstanding individual players and with a commitment to attack whenever that was possible. The Danish team were out, but they took enormous credit back home with them from this game.

Within 24 hours the semi-finalists were decided: Croatia scored a stunning 3–0 shock victory over Germany; while the Dutch took out Argentina in a controversial game in Marseille.

The Croats, who were the surprise team of the tournament, were too strong for the ageing German side and their players reacted powerfully to the pre-match propaganda from the Germans which had written them off. Their Real Madrid striker,

Davor Suker, snapped angrily: 'The German coach, Bertie Vogts, said before the game that this was David v Goliath and that was an insult to us and our nation. We were not going to forget that, nor forgive it. We went into the game playing from our hearts.'

The bad feeling between the two countries had lingered on after Germany defeated them en route to ultimate victory in Euro '96. The Croatians lost in the Old Trafford quarter-final and had harboured a grudge since. This time they won and won comfortably with goals from Robert Jarni, Goran Vlaiovic and Suker.

Afterwards, Derby County defender Igor Stimac insisted: 'We spent the last two years thinking about this day, the day when we would defeat Germany. The Germans did not respect us in England and they did not respect us here in France and we have given them their answer. We are a new country with only four million people and we are playing for each one of the Croatian citizens. For 45 years we could not call ourselves Croats because we were just a part of Yugoslavia and now that has changed and it is so very, very important for all of us.'

In Marseille, Argentina lost to Holland and Daniel Passarella admitted: 'We had always held the fear that the game against England had drained our players both mentally and physically. That is what happened. We could not lift the players for another supreme effort so soon. Because of the way the fixtures worked out we had a day less than the Dutch to rest, that can be crucial in this kind of competition. It was too much for us.'

Patrick Kluivert scored for Holland early in the game and Claudio Lopez equalised soon after. The game remained undecided until the last minute, when Denis Bergkamp scored. It was marred earlier, though, when Ariel Ortega was ordered off after head-butting the Dutch veteran keeper Edwin van der Sar. He had to go, but the Argentinian did have a grievance as he had been hacked down moments earlier by Jaap Stam in an incident which should have brought the South Americans a penalty. Then, to rub salt into their wounds and further feed their paranoia that no one really liked them in world football, Bergkamp scored minutes later, only seconds before the final whistle. Yet the Arsenal striker should have been ordered off against Yugoslavia after a stamping incident which the match officials then had ignored. It was rough justice, though Holland played the better and more dangerous football on the day and their win was deserved. It catapulted them into a confrontation with Brazil, while the hosts, France, were asked to face Croatia. In the days between qualification and the matches, it was Guus Hiddink who took on the role of chief critic of the champions, as he compared them unfavourably with the Brazil of old. As he waited for the match in Marseille, Hiddink, who claimed to have been inspired by the Brazilians in his own coaching career, could not help himself pointing out: 'Brazil have altered their basic approach recently. They are not as artistic as they once were. Instead, they have become functional as a team and now they grind out their results without the flair you always look for from their players. In fact, if anything, we play less defensively than they do. I want my teams to play as the old Brazil teams did and so we go forward and attack as often as we can. It is that way that football is a spectacle, a game that the supporters want to see. There is no way in the world that I shall change my thought on the game now. My beliefs were inspired by the way Brazil once played and if I abandon my ideals and play defensively then the people of Holland will not forgive me and they would be right.'

Both teams were feeling the effects of the tournament by now, with Arthur Numan and Winston Bogarde out through injury and Marc Overmars could only make a place on the bench. Brazil were missing the suspended Cafu and Mario Zagallo was now clearly feeling the pressure. He had cut short his press conference after the win over Denmark, and now he faced another stern challenge from Europe.

Four years earlier Brazil had defeated the Dutch 3–2 in the quarter-finals in the United States but it had been a close-run thing and the central defender Aldair admitted ahead of the game: 'Holland have grown in power in the last four years since we last met.' And Leonardo added tellingly: 'They have been able to persuade their individual players to adjust and play with the others, which has strengthened the team as a collective force. Holland have always been able to produce wonderful individual players but now, also, they are playing more as a team than they did four years ago.'

It was an epic collision and one which saw the two teams level at 1–1 after 90 minutes and heading for yet another set of penalties to decide who went on to the final. Ronaldo had scored a glorious goal as the match moved into the second half, and that was only cancelled out when Patrick Kluivert equalised in the eighty-seventh minute. Both countries had opportunities for the 'golden goal' in the extra time, but almost inevitably the game went into a shoot-out. And here the veteran Brazilian keeper Taffarel was the hero for the South Americans. As his team-mates Ronaldo, Rivaldo, Emerson and Dunga all scored, he saved twice – from Philip Cocu and from Ronald de Boer – and it was Brazil who were set to move onwards to Paris and the final.

'Penalties,' said de Boer afterwards, 'are a lottery. It is terrible to go out of the World Cup in this way. For us the dream is over.'

As with England, the Dutch had crashed out of Euro '96 in similar fashion and Hiddink conceded defiantly: 'It would be easy to hide behind excuses but I will not do that. To search for excuses would be a mistake. I was satisfied with the performance of my team, until it came to the penalties. In the 90 minutes and in the extra period we played well and that is all I can ask for from the players. It just did not turn out right for us at the end.'

Now Brazil were through. Now Brazil were in the final and the onus was on the French to provide the 'dream clash' the host country had looked for since the tournament kicked off. The French had always wanted to see their team face the World Cup holders in the final, now only Croatia stood between them and that game.

Unfortunately, the Croatians were determined to spoil the party. They had arrived unsung and unheralded and they had their dream. Their coach, Miroslav Blazevic, played the patriot card quite shamelessly. He knew that his team would be underdogs yet again as they walked out on to the field at Stade de France with *La Marseillaise* roaring down at them from the great stands and echoing out into the Paris suburb of St-Denis, as the French fans psyched up their own players for the semi-final clash.

And so Blazevic insisted: 'I said from the beginning of the tournament that it was our destiny to be in this game – and also in the final. There is no great secret to what we do in the Croatian team. Our strength lies in our unity, the spirit we have in our squad is the same as the spirit which binds our country. But in this game we cannot allow these emotions to be uppermost in our minds, we must think clearly about what we have to do against France. We neutralised the German team in the quarter-final and that has to happen again here if we are to go on and face the Brazilians. But, remember, the French team must also find ways of stopping Croatia playing. We have attacking, creative players who can trouble them, and I am sure Aime Jacquet will be preparing right now with that thought in his mind.'

The French were not treating their opponents lightly; they were not going to fall into the same trap as the Germans and dismiss them beforehand as an obstacle which was there simply to be swept aside by a superior force. As their experienced defender Laurent Blanc stressed: 'They may be a young nation, but already they have shown themselves to be a great footballing nation. I always thought that there would be one surprise in the last four, one unexpected team who would get to this stage. And I thought that it would be either Yugoslavia or Croatia who would be that team.

'It was my feeling because the two countries have always had such talented footballers. And Croatia, though one of the emerging nations in Eastern Europe, have always enjoyed a rich tradition in the game because, for many years, the Croatian players were the outstanding stars in the Yugoslav international teams. Look at the players they have – they play with the best clubs all around Europe. We know that and we respect that and, as far as the players are concerned, this is going to be as tough a game as any we have had to face already on the way to this semi-final.'

So said Blanc, and Jacquet was in the same mood, there would be no over-confidence apparent when the French went into action, they could not be allowed that kind of indulgence in any case because their goal-scoring worries were still there to haunt them. Missed chances had been a feature of their play and Jacquet ordered his front men to watch video footage of the misses they had racked up and declared: 'They have to learn from the mistakes they have been making. This has been happening too often and it has made it difficult for the team. We don't want to rely on another golden goal or on penalty kicks, we want to win outright without any additional problems. If we are to do that then we shall have to start to turn our territorial advantage into the goals which our play has earned – but which we have not been able to score. That has to change if we are to reach the final or if, even, we are going to be able to win the trophy.'

The players delivered for Jacquet as their uneasy progress towards the finishing line became a triumphant march to meet the Brazilians – even though they had gone a goal behind after their offside trap had failed them.

That happened only half a minute after the second half had started. The French defence, normally so highly disciplined, moved out as Alijosa Asanovic played the ball forward towards Davor Suker. Somehow, though, the right-back Lilian Thuram had reacted more slowly than his colleagues. He sat in and Suker was played on side and he was able to strike a shot from close range beyond Fabian Barthez.

The crowd was silenced – apart, that is, from their own tiny band of followers. This was exactly the tragedy Jacquet had wanted to avoid, the kind of elementary mistake he knew that the Croatians would punish. He held his head in his hands as if unable to believe what he had seen and then, suddenly, Thuram, the 26-year-old who played with Parma in Italy's Serie A, decided to take matters into his own hands and to make amends. Inside a minute he stormed forward out of defence, dispossessed Zvonimir Boban on the 18-yard line and when that ball broke clear he was in position to take a pass from Youri Djorkaeff and send a fiercely angled shot out of the reach of Drazen Ladic and into the net. In 69 minutes Thuram, playing like a man possessed, scored a follow-up goal. This time he powered his way past a challenge from Zvonimir Soldo inside the penalty box and struck another fierce drive past Ladic, that was the goal which sealed victory. There was more incident before the end – as tension grew palpably on and off the field. With 15 minutes left to play, Laurent Blanc, the rock at the very heart of the French defence, was red-carded after clashing with the Everton player Slaven Bilic. The Frenchman aimed a punch at his opponent as they jostled each other, the Croatian went down and the referee brought out his red card and France were down to ten men.

The time between the sending-off of Blanc and the final whistle was a nervous and edgy one for the French players and the French support. But they survived, and after being semi-finalists on three previous occasions – in Sweden in 1958, in Spain in 1982 and in Mexico 1986 – they at last reached the place in the final they had wanted so desperately. It was a deserved victory but it had come at a cost, with Blanc now unavailable for the biggest game in his life and in his country's history. Afterwards, Jacquet admitted Blanc's absence could be critical when he said: 'He is a very important player for us and now we shall have to make changes and that is not what you want as you go into the final of the World Cup. I do not believe that the player deserved a red card; he has never been in trouble like this before in his career. It is terrible for France and even more terrible for Laurent Blanc that he will not be back in the stadium for the final. That is a tragedy, especially after all he has done in the tournament. Now we are to face the masters of the game and we know how difficult it will be for us. Brazil appear to have improved after every game they have played and to beat Denmark and then Holland demonstrates just how strong they have become. But no one should forget that we are home. Even Brazil will not be able to relax knowing that we have the people with us. That is now going to be a very vital factor for our players and they know that. The country is with us, they were willing us to victory today and they will be doing the same in the final and we must respond, we cannot let them down now. We have to win the World Cup for France and we have to win it for Laurent Blanc, now, as well. We are here to make history, Brazil know that.'

Before that, though, the French decided it was time to flex their muscles as hosts of the tournament and began to exert pressure on FIFA in a bid to overturn the automatic suspension which would keep Laurent Blanc out of the game. Television showed that the contact made by Blanc with Bilic had been minimal and the Croatian was being pilloried as a cheat. Blanc, who had never been sent off at club level or in 73 international appearances, won the backing of the French Federation as they considered an appeal, but their efforts were in vain. The governing body would not change the rules – even for the French – and in a terse statement issued 72 hours before the final they made their position plain. It read simply: 'There is no appeal possible against a one- or two-game ban. Only when the FIFA disciplinary body judges a three-game ban is necessary for the specific offence can an appeal be lodged. On this occasion the relevant committee does not have the power to lift the ban. The only way Laurent Blanc could be available for the final is if there had been a case of mistaken identity and he had not been involved in the incident. There is no other avenue open.'

While Aime Jacquet talked of an appeal the player himself was less sanguine concerning the outcome. Shrugging, he commented briefly at the team's headquarters: 'It would be a great surprise to me if the suspension was lifted on this occasion even though I feel it is unjust. But it has never been done before and this would be unique and I do not see FIFA taking that kind of action just before the World Cup final. My expulsion punishes me as a player, but it also punishes the whole team and I am left feeling that I have tasted the cake but I am not allowed to touch the cherry.'

The other protagonist, Bilic, was less poetic in his assessment of the incident which had now become a full-blown scandal in the French media. The Everton player, who is also a lawyer, declared: 'I did not get him sent off. He did that all by himself. He touched me with his hand in the face and that is an offence and the referee saw it. I am not happy that he is going to miss the final, but other than that this has nothing to do with me. We were all warned as players what would happen at these finals if you raised your hands and he knew that as well as all the rest of us. It was always going to be the case that you would be punished. There were enough warnings from FIFA before and during the finals to remind every player of the consequences of lifting your hands to an opponent. It was very well documented.'

Bilic, though, took his share of criticism as the furore over diving gained force because of the publicity which was focused on the semi-final clash. There had been other incidents of 'cheating' at the finals and the referees had been warned to clamp down on that particular problem before the group games had been completed; for example, Pierre van Hooijdonk, the Dutch striker, had been yellow-carded for diving in the other semi-final against Brazil when he appeared as a substitute.

The real concern for France and their coach Aime Jacquet was that Blanc was such an inspirational figure in the team that he was perceived to be almost irreplaceable by the supporters. And while that was surely enough to give Jacquet sleepless nights before the Brazil game, there was still the failure of his front players to get goals. They had scored against the lesser opposition of Saudi Arabia and South Africa when their bid for glory had begun, but since the section games the goals from the strikers had dried up, and against Paraguay it had been Laurent Blanc's 'golden goal' which had prevailed, while against Italy there had been the penalty shoot-out, and then against Croatia it had been the right-back Lilian Thuram who had come to his country's rescue with two memorable strikes. The question constantly addressed to Jacquet was why the men up front had failed so frequently; he attempted to answer it with a tactical logic which may have convinced his fellow coaches in France and may also have comforted his under-fire strike force, but it did not completely satisfy the press or the man in the street.

Jacquet's argument was this: 'The strength of the team is in the way we play for each other. This is a collective effort and we are achieving our objectives by sheer force of will on occasions. People are making far too much of the fact that the front players have not been scoring. It does not concern me who gets the goals for the team, just as long as the goals come. It was no surprise to the coaching staff with the team that Lilian Thurman scored the two goals in the semi-final against Croatia, because he is always encouraged to push forward and to play as a wing-back when we have possession. He did that to perfection in our last game and it underlined that the overall contribution is what matters most to us. There are no divisions within the squad. It is the very heart of the team where we see our strength. Even without getting goals the front players have done their jobs by making space for others, and as long as that happens again in the final then I shall be happy. I refuse to let this become a major issue because, and I'm being honest here, I do not see it that way.

'Every single player has made his contribution to our reaching the final, that is how we look at things with the squad and how we will look at things after the tournament has been completed. We were brought together by the criticism we have all had to suffer, and that has been an important factor in what we have so far achieved. I think it is always the case that a group can be brought closer together in adversity. Our belief in what we were doing was strengthened by the many harsh things which were said about us during our preparations and even when the games in these finals started. Some people did not understand what we were doing and so they were dismissive. But we all believed.'

It was that belief which had sustained Jacquet, his backroom staff and his players from some cruel criticisms, and even on the eve of the final there were those who refused to believe that the French could raise their game to defeat the Brazilians and bring the trophy back to its founder's home. While the holders remained favourites there seemed to be a feeling that victory for France would be a poetic justice – given the contribution of Rimet and the support the country had given the tournament since its birth in the early '30s.

Pele, that legendary figure – whose presence still lights up whatever gathering he joins at major tournaments around the globe – gave his support to his own country, pushing aside the unhappiness which he had expressed back in Rio when he was reported as saying that Holland would win the competition. He laughed that off by explaining: 'I admire Holland and their players and their approach to the game – and I would always say that, but I would never place them ahead of my own country. Now I think that Brazil will win, but I also think that this might be one of the great finals and I do not see it being one of these games which must be decided in extra time or with penalties. This is a game where we shall know the winners over the regulation 90 minutes. I think that France have problems about getting goals, while, apart from the Norway game, Brazil have simply improved and looked ever more dangerous as the World Cup has progressed.'

For Mario Zagallo – the man so many Brazilians had wished to see sacked after the embarrassing run of results suffered in the CONCACAF Gold Cup in the United States and whose own Federation president had foisted Zico on him as his technical assistant – there had been considerable vindication of his tactics and his team selections. Now he stood ready to take part in his *fifth* World Cup final – he had been a member of the victorious 1958 side in Sweden alongside Pele and was there again in Chile in 1962 and was manager in 1970 when Brazil triumphed in Mexico; following that he was assistant to Carlos Alberto Parreira in USA '94 when Brazil had been victorious once more. Some of the strain had been wiped from his face after the trauma of the Denmark game, he assessed the final and pointed out: 'I do not see the point in going back over all the other finals I have been involved in. It is not the right thing to do, to compare previous teams with the present players. In any case, I have found something different to savour at all five of the finals I have been involved in. Once you have the taste, you always want more and it has been that way for me and now, here I am, in another final when so many had written me off.

'The critics will come out again if we lose, but we are not thinking about that. We respect France but we do not fear them. We, as a nation, have been in too many finals, too many big games to approach them with any apprehension. This is our fifth World Cup final and only the first for the French and that will count in our favour.'

Zagallo, though, was soon to find that the tension in his team was to hit his hopes and end his dreams of glory, while the French, lifted by the occasion, by the support and by the fervour which gripped the country, were to triumph.

On that evening Zinedine Zidane scored twice in the first half with headers while the Brazil defence watched, unable to mark him when the crosses came over. And then, in injury time, Emmanuel Petit snatched a third and Brazil had lost and the inquests bagan. Of course, Ronaldo was at the centre of them all. The Inter Milan striker had not been listed in the team sheets when they were handed to the world's press half an hour before the game. Then, soon afterwards, just before kick-off, his name was there and he took the field, but his contribution was small. Afterwards, Zagallo was grilled by the Brazilian newsmen as to what had happened. In front of our eyes, Zagallo rounded on the writers who had been savaging him on an almost daily basis over the months leading up to the finals. Furiously he answered them, snapping: 'Ronaldo was not a hundred per cent fit, it is as simple as that. We left the decision to play him until close to the kick-off because we had genuine concerns about his readiness to play in the final. It was a severe psychological blow to our team. The other players worried about Ronaldo before the game because of his condition.

'And they worried about him during the game, too, because there were fears that he might break down. He played in the game because he was important to the team and I am here to tell you that. I am a man and I am here to face all of you and to tell you that. We knew that we needed Ronaldo and then we decided that he should be in the team because of his value and because the French feared him. I do not think we had any alternative at all.'

Then he added: 'The game was over for us in that first half. I just wanted that first 45 minutes to end because we lost two goals in the air and that had been the same story against Holland. Zidane did well, but he should have been stopped. It was obvious after the first goal, but then we repeated the mistake and when you do that then it is difficult to come back. Today, for us, it was impossible to hit back, even though we did better in the second period of the game. The final belonged to the French at the end and I will say no more than that.'

If Zagallo reacted angrily then his opposite number, Aime Jacquet, was equally unforgiving to his enemies, stating forcibly: 'Some of the lies told about this team have been shameless. There are journalists in France who have been against us from the beginning, but tonight we proved what we could do. We knew the nation was behind us. When we left the hotel training camp to come to the stadium they were in the streets to cheer us, and when we arrived it was the same and that was so important to us. We knew then that we had to win the trophy for the people of France. Tonight we played as well as we did at any time in the tournament. There were some little adjustments we had to make to our tactics to handle Brazil and these worked and that is how we were able to win.

'Brazil gave us an enormous test of character because we were all aware that we were facing the champions, but we came through and this has been the greatest night in the history of French football. Nothing has ever been better, nothing can match this.'

Meanwhile, Paris came to a standstill, the city was *en fête* and transport ground to a halt. It was almost four o'clock in the morning before I made it back to my hotel through the crowds thronging the streets in celebration. The Brazilians, however, returned to their hotel to talk long into the night over the Ronaldo affair.

It was only the following morning that the truth emerged, and the world learned that the young striker's room-mate, Roberto Carlos, had awakened during the night to find the Inter Milan player having a convulsion. And how, after treatment in hospital, Ronaldo was allowed to rejoin the squad and was eventually given medical permission to play. But the illness affected him and his team-mates, and while no one can grudge the French their success – after all, they were missing Laurent Blanc it must be remembered – the whole Ronaldo mystery did contribute to the lifeless display given by Brazil in the period before half-time when, really, the final was decided and the destination of the trophy confirmed. The debate continues in Rio; but in France the victory is all that matters. The trophy had gone home at last, back to France, back to the country where Jules Rimet floated the idea which has now grown into the greatest sporting event in the world. France were worthy winners and they proved yet again that the team which peaks at the right time is always liable to be winners. They peaked that night and it counted.

Epilogue

Some months after the World Cup had ended, the Scotland manager Craig Brown, now starting a European Championship campaign, reflected on what might have been and what changes he would have made, if any, in the way of personnel and preparation.

'It is difficult to see what else we could have done,' he mused, 'except, of course, win that last game and come home with an enhanced reputation. But when I think it all through and – as you will imagine – I have done that frequently over the weeks and months since France, I don't see that I would have changed things all that much. There was, for example, nothing wrong with the programme we put in place as a build-up to the finals. The warm-up games were those we wanted, because I had decided that we did not want any easy games, and while that might not look good on the CV, because we did not get a win in any of them, people have to look more deeply into things. We lost to Denmark, and we saw how well they played when they were in France. Then we drew with Finland – when we played what was essentially a weakened team – and, in any case, Finland are no mugs, they came close to qualification for France, remember. Then, in the United States we drew with Colombia and the United States of America who were also in the finals in France. Plus we played these two countries in searing heat in New York and Washington and that was designed to help our fitness levels in the finals and it worked.

'We may not have been able to win any of the games, but we did have a squad as fit as any of the others who were in France. You saw that against Norway and some of their people had questioned our ideas about going abroad. Well, we knew what had worked for us before and we thought it would work again and it did, and given a few breaks, it would have worked for us if we had gone further in the tournament. I mean, as well as playing the games in

131

that heat – and you were talking a hundred degrees in Washington – we were also training very hard and very seriously. You are not talking about some kind of holiday jaunt.'

It was there in the States, too, that the passing, patient, possession game the Scots had been intent on developing, flourished. Against Colombia, the South Americans simply found themselves unable to get the ball, something they had so often been able to do when they were playing against British teams.

Brown explained: 'I think that we played as well as we have ever done in that game in New York. It was so unusual for a British team to be able to do that against the South Americans. We surprised them and I think we surprised the Brazilians in the opening match, too, because of our approach. They were not looking for us to play in that way any more than the Colombians had been.

'In a way we can take some little bit of satisfaction from that. We did develop a style of play which so many people admired. And it was one which suited the players we had with us. It had taken some time for everything to work out right for us but it did and I think, perhaps, the fact that both John Collins and Paul Lambert had picked up experience on the continent helped our cause. The spell with Monaco allowed John to see how the patient approach worked and it was the same with Paul at Dortmund. It is not the kind of thing you see in the Premier League at home.

'Nor do you see it in England. The pace of the game in Britain is hectic and the supporters are used to that and so are the players, so we need the help of John and Paul to re-educate the players to some extent. It was the same with the defensive set-up which I employed with the side, from my first time in charge. I thought it was right for the players I could call on and I thought, too, that it was the right play for international level. If you look at the statistics of the World Cup you will find that 24 out of 32 teams who were taking part used the three-at-the-back system. That is a set-up which has served us well and we have been using it for around five years now and it is the way we want to continue, except when specific games might call for a change. But I feel that we were ahead of the game in that one. A lot of other countries have picked up on that way of playing after we did. It does suit our personnel and it has been good for us. It has made it difficult for teams to score goals against the team and I think some of the Norway players commented on that after the game in Bordeaux.

That was a nice little tribute for us, even though it did not help us to qualify.'

Brown still feels, even months afterwards, a sense of injustice as he studies the tapes of the games over and over again. He was reticent at the time over the refereeing decision which went against his side, but after detailed examination of the video evidence he concludes: 'We should have had three penalties instead of just the one we were awarded against Brazil. Late in the game Dunga handled a John Collins free-kick; then Gordon Durie was brought down inside the penalty box against Norway and not outside – but, of course, the kick was given outside the box; and then there was another penalty that we should have been given against Morocco. I still believe that if one of these had gone our way then we would have qualified, which is what we wanted to do for all these supporters who were in France and for all the people at home who gave us their backing. But it was not to be, unfortunately.

'The Morocco game was one of the strangest I have ever been involved in. When you go over the statistics you find that we had by far the bulk of the play, you find that we had more attacking moves than they did, you find we had five corners to their one and that we had 22 shots to their 14. Interestingly enough, I have given out these match facts to other coaches without saying which teams were involved and then I have asked them who they thought won the match. To a man they have all answered that Scotland were winners, when I tell them which game the facts came from then they are amazed. It was not so much that we played badly throughout the game, it was just that we did make errors and we were punished for them. You know, looking at the game again, we even had more of the play in the 25 minutes we were left with only ten men.'

As for criticism over personnel, Brown answers simply: 'Even with the value of hindsight I would not have chosen Ally McCoist at that time. I have picked him since but his own circumstances at club level have changed now. He is in the Kilmarnock team and playing regularly and scoring goals. When I was naming the squad he was not playing in every game for Rangers and they even left him out of their Scottish Cup final starting line-up. That is what I looked at and thought hard about before leaving him out.

'It was not an easy decision to make, but it was one I had to reach and, on the evidence, I still believe I was right. As for the poeple who keep telling me that the squad was too old they should look at the others. We were not the oldest squad at the tournament, the Germans were, and there were others older than we were. Also, I think if you took the ages of all the squads you would find that there were a considerable number of 30-somethings around in France. You cannot pack an international team with youngsters, you need experience when you get to that level. I will bring in young players when appropriate, but throwing in too many at a major tournament is not the way to go about this job. Other coaches obviously agree with me, when you see the average age of most of the teams who took part. Actually, you will find that the majority of players who were in France are between 27 and 31. We were not very much out of step at all.

'Honestly, if we had had just a little luck then we would have been in Marseille playing Italy, and we might even had managed to go a little further. The record books will show us with just one point, but we performed much better than the results show and I think everyone who was there – and I include our opponents and the neutrals – would agree with me on that. I think the football we played in our first two games added quality to the tournament and showed the world that even if we cannot qualify we can still play good intelligent football. That is some consolation when we look back at the finals. I only wish we could have given the Tartan Army a little more to celebrate. They deserved that, every last one of them.'

PART II

IN STEP WITH THE TARTAN ARMY

Tom Shields

France '98 Diary

Saturday, 12 October 1997

The road to France '98 starts with a kiss. Not from a fragrant mademoiselle but from an unsavoury Highlander reeking of BO and drink. The scene is Celtic Park where Scotland are playing Latvia in the last qualifying match. Despite sitting bang in the centre of Parkhead's brand new stand I have a restricted view. This is not due to a stanchion or other structure; it is due to the Pipe Band from Hell.

They are an unofficial ensemble, all painted faces and outfits out of the menswear section of Tam Shepherd's Joke Shop. The pipe major sports a *Hagar the Horrible* tartan hat with plastic horns. He wields a plastic mace, constructed in best Blue Peter style. And he does wield it. A band follower whose behaviour fell below the required standards received a warning clunk on the head. They are a lovely bunch of people, but the only problem is that I'm sitting two rows behind them and when they stand up to play you can't see the match. Especially when the drunken Highlander right in front stands on his seat so that he can see over the pipe band.

I am a card-carrying coward but finally decide that enough is enough and give the Highlander a substantial dunt in the back. Just as I do so, Gordon Durie scores the second goal. The Highlander turns round, hugs me and gives me a slobbering and very alcoholic kiss.

The band and sundry other kilted fans are involved in a pile-up during the celebrations of the goal. It is a terrible tangle in the passageway. Believe me, until you've seen a dozen kilted chaps go head over heels, you have not seen one of the more challenging sights in football. But, as we sing along with Doris Day: 'Que será

137

será, whatever will be will be, we're going to gay Paree', I know that for the first time in my life I'm going to see Scotland in the World Cup finals.

Sunday, 13 October 1997

I start my research for France '98 with a piece of essential reading: Hugh Johnson's *Pocket Wine Book*. After all, no self-respecting Scottish football fan wants to turn up in France next summer not knowing their Fleurie from their Fitou.

Wine and fitba gang thegither as Robert Burns might have said, if only football had been invented when he was a boy. At least Kilmarnock might have had some decent lyrics for their songs.

But, back to the wine. The Caronne-Ste-Gemme sounds appropriate for any Scots fan. From the St Laurent area of Bordeaux it has a 'steady, stylish quality which repays patience'. A bit like the Scottish team.

As a tribute to our team coach you could try a drop of Cantenac-Brown, also from Bordeaux, which is described as 'formerly old-fashioned but promising since 1994'. Similarly, in honour of a certain player's half-centenary of caps, we could raise a glass of Boyd-Cantenac. It is an 'attractive wine, full of flavour'.

Individual performances by some of the Scottish players may drive the fans to sample La Clotte, a pungent and supple St Emilion. A poor display by the entire team could be marked by quaffing a bottle of Le Crock, a particularly fine *cru bourgeois* from St Estephe in the Bordeaux region.

Decisions by referees can be celebrated, or otherwise, with some of the products of Kuentz-Bas, a top-quality house in Alsace. Finally, a little number which might be appropriate should the thoughts of any member of the Tartan Army stray from the football to *les belles filles*. It is called Clos de Tart, a Burgundy which the wine guide describes as 'at best wonderfully fragrant, young or old'.

November 1997

David Ross, a regular correspondent to the *Herald Diary*, suggests it is time I started brushing up my French for Scots football fans at the World Cup.

Top of the list is a cry we might expect to hear from Frank McAvennie: *Où sont les oiseaux?* On the same subject is the the traditional chat-up line: *Je suppose que mon trou est dehors de la question?*

If, by ill luck, Scots fans should get involved in a spot of bother they can tell the French polis: *Ils l'ont commencé pas nous.* Which means they started it, not us.

If, by chance, a fan has had too much to drink the night before, a hangover cure can be sought by either: *Où puis-je trouver de l'Irn Bru?* or *Où puis-je trouver quelque chose pour guerir ma guele de bois?* The latter translates very roughly as: Where might I find a refreshing soft drink? My gub is like the bottom of a budgie's cage.

December 1997
The draw: we've got Brazil, for a change, Norway and Morocco. No one said it was going to be easy.

January 1998
Ian and Alan Adie, two enterprising fans, have registered the words Tartan Army as a trademark. I see their photie in the newspaper. They are the Pipe Band from Hell which I met at Celtic Park. Their official name is the Wee-ist Pipe Band in the World. No marks for spelling, but top of the class for entrepreneurship.

February
The hunt for tickets begins.

March
The hunt for tickets continues.

April
Still not a hint of a ticket.

May
The SFA Travel Club write to say that my years of membership and attendance at Scotland matches qualifies me for a ticket for the opening game against Brazil.

Wednesday, 2 June
That magic moment when my ticket for the Brazil–Scotland match popped through the letterbox. So long a dream, the World Cup was becoming a reality. My own ticket, my own seat for the opening game of France '98 in the Stade de France.

I studiously ignore comments from those not of a footballing mind who look at the ticket's face value of £133 and ask: 'Does that include the return flight, accommodation, and full board?' Try to explain that footballing history does not come cheap.

The accompanying letter from *le petit caporal* – Monsieur Jim Farry of the SFA – slightly spoils the moment. In his note, M. Farry feels obligated to point out the importance of keeping the ticket in a safe place at all times.

In some detail *le petit caporal* explained that if you lose your your ticket, or if it somehow becomes damaged, there can be no replacements. If anything happens to your ticket, you will not get into the Grande Gemme on 10 June. It is being so cheerful that keeps M. Farry going. He adds: 'I hope that you have a wonderful time at the World Cup.'

Thursday, 3 June

At last, a World Cup prediction we can trust. It is from Frank McAvennie: 'My heart says Scotland, my head says Brazil, but my nose says Colombia.' This is not the real Frank McAvennie speaking, to let you understand, but the 'Where's the burdz?' TV persona as portrayed by Jonathon Watson in *Only an Excuse?*. Tosh McKinlay has been plucked from obscurity to be caricatured: 'It is not just an honour for myself,' he says, 'it is an honour for my club – Celtic reserves.'

• The Tartan Navy was a concept born in 1978 with those rumours of a submarine voyage to the World Cup in Argentina. It became a reality when fans sailed to the Faroe Islands in 1995. That was when the Scots commented upon the Faroese custom of slaughtering pilot whales by marching through the streets clutching inflatable dolphins and chanting: 'We're the famous Tartan Army and we're here to save the whale.'

There were reports of a Tartan Navy at Euro '96 when Scottish fans travelled by canal longboat. But the Tartan Navy were definitely in evidence when the good ship *Friendly Isle* docked in Glasgow on its way to France '98. The skipper is Oban fisherman Alasdair 'More Steam' MacPhail who was engineer on the legendary Park Bar Scotland supporters bus.

Someone said Alasdair's Tartan Navy is simply the Park Bar bus afloat. I do not recall the Park Bar bus being anything but afloat. By sheer chance a drinks company, Bilgewater Gin, is a sponsor of the

Tartan Navy. Ken Grant, co-skipper of the *Friendly Isle* launched Bilgewater as a protest against the trend by big distillers to produce ever weaker brands of gin. Bilgewater is 43 per cent and is blended to Ken's own specification in Invergordon. There is a wee party on board, with a few drinks, and the first casualty of the World Cup. A friend of the skipper who had come merely to see him off, slips on the quayside and ends up in stictches at the Western Infirmary.

• Reader Gordon Black is on the e-mail to say the reason for Brazil's success over the years, apart from the fact that they are simply better than everyone else, is that their players have great names. If we can't match them in sheer skill we can at least make an effort on the name front. He urges Craig Brown to field the following team against Brazil: Bandio, Boydio, Mattellio, Carlos Hendry, Calderado, Johnco, Toothtao, Paulo Lamberto, Kevincha, Durzinho, Bebootho. Substitutes would include Gemmillson (Archie's boy) and Didi (pick your own).

Friday, 5 June

Jim Farry's régime at the SFA has long stood accused of lacking a sense of humour. But the *bon voyage* pack for France-bound members of the SFA Travel Club goes some way to dispel this, particularly the wee badges which were enclosed.

The badge is a cut-out caricature of a Scots fan complete with a shock of ginger 'Jimmy' hair. It bears the message: 'Oui, mes amis, I won't let the side down.'

The pack also included a booklet of football terms and phrases in French. We find useful words like *malchance* (bad luck) and *eliminé* (eliminated), but not, for some reason, that essential Scottish World Cup phrase, goal difference. More positive is the inclusion of the verb *se qualifier*. Under the heading of fans, the list goes from applause, atmosphere, and banner (*applaudir, l'ambiance* and *un drapeau*) to wig (*perruque*). Under stadium-safety we have alcohol and ambulance (*l'alcool* and *une ambulance*) and hot water (*eau chaude*). For those who find themselves in eau chaude, the appropriate phrase is: '*Excusez-moi, je suis écossais.*'

Handy medical terms include dehydration (*la déshydratation*), head wound (*une blessure à la tete*), and stitches (*des points*). With luck the points will be won on the park and not inserted in casualty.

• There appears to be some confusion over the French for 'Where's the burdz?' An early version has it as '*Où sont les oiseaux?*' But no less an authority than Alistair McCoist, in a sketch filmed for his McCoist and MacAulay TV show, has it as '*Où sont les poulets?*'

Saturday, 6 June

The progress of the Tartan Navy, aka the trawler *Friendly Isle*, is being charted in a most hi-tech manner. First Metro Independent, a Glasgow-based Internet publisher, has Jamie Wilson, a young cybernaut on board who will file pictures and reports from sea and Seine. Ian Munro and the other veterans of World Cup travel, immediately nickname him Spidey because he is always on the Web.

Alasdair 'More Steam' MacPhail, skipper of the *Friendly Isle*, is less hi-tech, operating on intuition and many cups of strong coffee. In fact, when I contacted him by ship-to-shore radio to ask his position, he replied: 'We're aboot here.' Alasdair is from Islay.

Sunday, 7 June

Arrive in Paris, abandon car and go in search of the World Cup experience. The Auld Alliance bar, which has received so much publicity, is jammed full. An overspill bar is found a hundred yards away. The Bar Chiminere is quiet at about 8 p.m. and the *patron* is happy to see a half-dozen Scots provide some Sunday evening trade. At 10 p.m. there are at least 50 kilted ones and the *patron* is looking harassed and worried about the noisy singing. The turning point comes when a party of Borders Tartan Army chaps order a particularly large and, for the *patron*, lucrative rake of drink; as he pours the litres of beer at well over a fiver a time. By midnight, the *patron* has had a conversion of Damascus-road porportions. He is wearing a Jimmy hat and joins in a chorus of that wee song about Jimmy Hill.

• Members of the Tartan Army I meet are understandably nervous about having a representative of Her Majesty's press in their midst scribbling notes. 'Remember, Tam,' says Jim, who is a large chap working in the demolition industry and must be listened to. 'What happens in France, stays in France.' I promise my dispatches will be duly censored by a Tartan Army intelligence officer and authorised for sending back from the front line.

Not that there is much in the way of truly bad behaviour to report. There has been much flashing of what is underneath the kilt but this has been mostly at the request of the world's TV crews. Portuguese TV have brought along their own lovely Brazilian lady to be filmed with the Scots at the Bar Chiminere, but the lady refuses to get out of the car. 'I can see 12 pi-pis,' she said. 'I am staying in the car.' One of the pi-pis on display was that of a Frenchman who frequents the bar. As the Scots upped their kilts, he dropped his breeks. His action was greeted by loud choruses of 'Wee man, wee man . . .'

• We hear the first of many hard-luck stories of those who never made it to the World Cup '98. There are some people sitting at home who could have been in Paris on an all-expenses-paid trip. They work in the upper echelons of Scottish Power and had been invited to the match by a major supplier. Their dreams were shattered when the top management at Scottish Power ruled that such hospitality was inappropriate and anyone going to Paris would have to pay their own way. The troops have taken this news very badly, especially since those who made the decree have just made loads of cash from preferential share issues.

• And the story of someone who was determined to make it to France '98, no matter what. Graeme, a young fan from Galashiels, went through a bit of a nightmare the day he was due to leave for Paris. He was working away on the farm, scouring the calves or something filthy and agricultural, but his thoughts were very much on the trip to the football which he had bought and paid for. He even had a ticket for the Brazil match, duly earned by his air miles as a member of the SFA Travel Club. It was during this reverie that a cow kicked him on the knee. He was carted off to hospital where his by now heavily-swollen knee was bandaged up. An understanding doctor decreed that Graeme would be as well hirpling about Paris as he would about Galashiels. 'I still can't bend my knee and I'm actually faster walking backwards,' said Graeme. Among the many bizarre sights to be seen in Paris, there is nothing stranger than a big Borders farm laddie in kilt and Scotland top being led backwards by his mates.

Monday, 8 June
French officialdom don't seem to have got the point yet about the

Scots fans. Like the man at the immigration desk at Charles de Gaulle airport who detained Davie from Dumbarton on the grounds that he didn't look like his passport photograph. Davie pointed out that it was not normal to have your passport photie taken wearing a huge floppy blue and white top hat and with a saltire painted on your face. The immigration official ordered Davie to remove the top hat. He did so to reveal a tartan bunnet with ginger Jimmy hair. The official gave in.

• I finally get a pint in the Auld Alliance pub through the good offices of owner Ronnie Brown, who passes on his thanks to *Herald Diary* readers. We had written in *The Diary* some three years before of his plan to open a pub in Paris called the Highlander's Howff. We applauded the concept but thought the name might be something of a stumbling block and asked readers to come up with a better one. The popular choice was the Auld Alliance, which has the definite plus point that his French customers can pronounce it. Ronnie has become the source in Paris for all things Scottish. Antoine, a nightclub owner, was in the Auld Alliance looking for help in finding a bagpiper for a Brazil–Scotland theme party after the match. Ronnie pointed out that most pipers would already be booked up, but he would see what he could do. The search for a volunteer was made slightly easier by the fact that the piper will have to share the stage with two acts called Gogo Girls Samba and the Pom-Pom Girls.

• It is getting a bit out of hand, this flashing of what is underneath the kilt. A flash which will surely become a video out-take collector's item is actor Ewan MacGregor revealing all during the recording of the McCoist and MacAulay TV show at the Eiffel Tower. It is fair to say that young Mr MacGregor was egged on to show his Eiffel by his dad, who also appeared on the show. Father Jim was first to raise his kilt, but he was wearing black boxer shorts. Ally McCoist presaged the moment by asking, in his unique interviewing style, if Ewan got his kit off in the movies because it was essential to the plot or was it because 'you have got a big knob?'. In further banter on the subject of Ewan's Eiffel, proud father Jim said: 'He takes it from his dad.' Fred MacAulay, renowned for his speed of riposte, said: 'I didn't know you were that close a family.' This programme is heading for more beeps than in a Jerry Springer show.

Richard Wilson, the faux lugubrious actor from Greenock, was in splendid form. 'I saw your acting in the clips,' he said to Ally and Fred, 'a load of shite'. Fred hinted that this was being a bit unfair to shite.

The show, recorded on the first floor of the Eiffel Tower in front of an audience of refreshed and frisky Scottish fans, had the potential to go into disastrous TV territory whence not even a Hogmanay show has ever gone. The first guest was Jimmy Hill, the man the Tartan Army loves, even lives, to hate. Justin, the programme director, came onstage to ask that the audience refrain from that wee chant about Mr Hill's alleged sexual orientation. 'If you do, it will be to the eternal disgrace of the Tartan Army and it will play into the hands of tabloid journalists,' he said.

But the fans were ahead of Justin. When Mr Hill came on, he was greeted with: 'We love Jimmy Hill, he's a god, he's a god.' The *bête noire* is in danger of becoming an icon. Jimmy was in conciliatory mode. He smarmed (okay, let's be charitable and say charmed) his way through the interview with some stuff about how sad he gets when Scotland go out the World Cup. The Tartan Army chaps in the audience were remarkably well behaved, even the guy in the front row with the knife through his head. Some of their impromptu contributions deserved to be kept in the show. Like the guy who shouted 'Ah want his job!' as a BBC technical person fumbled about the fabled chest of Ulrika Jonsson to attach a microphone. What has Ulrika got to do with World Cup football? Not a lot. She was there as token tottie and managed, while Jimmy Hill was busy earning his Scottish citizenship, to play the part of the condescending southerner.

• After the show, the celebs head to the Auld Alliance. The *Herald Diary* thought about joining them but went for a curry instead. (Yes, a curry in Paris. Yes, it was terrible.) Meanwhile, at the Auld Alliance, Ulrika was getting a non-PC doing from her footballer boyfriend Stan Collymore and *The Diary* had missed yet another exclusive.

• But we prefer observing the common man to celebrity-spotting. Like the two Paisley men who had just arrived in Paris and were settling down in a bar on the Grands Boulevards having ordered two giant litre glasses of lager. 'Twenty-five quid for two beers. That's a disgrace,' says one. Two or three sips into their beer, he says: 'Do you want a half to go with it, Hughie?' Two large whiskies are ordered bringing the price for their admittedly large haufs and haufs to £50.

• The Scots fans in Paris had gathered in some numbers under the Eiffel Tower for a beer, a kick about with a football and to harass in an amiable enough fashion any passing *oiseau*. There was singing too, of course, including one of the neatest ditties heard so far: 'Only a pylon, the Eiffel's only a pylon . . .'

Tuesday, 9 June

It has to be said that so far the French police have been magnificent in their treatment of the Scottish fans. During the opening parade celebrations, I chance upon a squad of the feared CRS riot police, in a sidestreet off the Champs-Elysées. Believe it or not, they have their own bar operating out of the back of one of their vans. One of the cops is willing enough to provide us with a beer or two, but his superior officer vetoed this on the grounds that they only have enough for themselves. Another riot police-man, meanwhile, is chatting up a female Scots fan, asking her for a light for his cigar and asking: 'Are you heated up for me?' The Paris police have been extremely patient with some of the excesses of the fans, and one of the sights of the week was the patrol car which cruised slow past the Auld Alliance bar with a member of the Tartan Army in full kit sitting on the roof.

• Overheard, a chap in a kilt who obviously wanted to make himself more attractive to the foreign TV crews, asking his pal: 'See when we get back to the hotel, will you paint a saltire on my arse?'

• Supporters from every competing nation (with thankfully few English) have gathered on the Champs-Elysées and Gary from Ayr has been busy cementing international relations. He is wearing a kilt, an Argentine top and a fez. Wherever there is a knot of fans, of whatever nationality, you are likely to find Gary in the middle leading the singing. When he's not singing on the Champs-Elysées he is singing round the bonfire in the campsite in the Bois de Boulogne.

When he's not singing, he is giving interviews to the TV stations of the world. He is becoming something of an expert broadcaster, delivering soundbites first-time. He would be as well staying up all night since he has to be on *The Big Breakfast*, or *Le Grand Petit Déjeuner* as they call it in Paris. Gary says he is having the best time of his life. His only regret is that his beloved girlfriend Linda is not here to share it with him. At least that's what he's going to tell *The Big Breakfast*.

• There is a swish and much-hyped eve-of-opening-match party at a place called the Buddha Bar, which is to be attended by a host of luminaries such as Sean Connery, Ewan MacGregor, Alex Salmond and maybe even Donald Dewar. It is a must to gatecrash for a newspaper diarist seeking juicy material. But the Champs-Elysées is too crowded to move. I find myself at the crossroads of two small streets off the boulevard.

The corner bars, and indeed the streets, are entirely occupied by Scottish fans. They are singing: 'Were the famous Tartan Army and we're here to save the snail . . .' The Parisians are bemused but they are beginning to smile at the antics of the Scots, even when they decide to sit down and block all traffic. One of the those sitting down is a young man wearing a kilt, a Brazilian jersey and a Jimmy hat. He appears to be of oriental extraction. Still thinking of the great internationalist overtones to the day, I approach and ask him how he comes to be supporting Scotland. 'Because I'm from Thurso. Do you know where Thurso is?' I retreat, thoroughly embarrassed at perpetrating an inverse form of racism, ashamed for forgetting that Jock Tamson's bairns come in many colours these days.

I am lucky later to get the benefit of an eyewitness report of the Buddha Bar bash. Our man in the inside was Tam Coyle of Glasgow. So just how glittering was it, Tam?

He says: 'The highlight for me was to stand at the next urinal to Sean Connery. Of course, I had a wee peek' he says.

And?

'Very impressive. Nearly as impressive as mine,' Tam says.

• The Tartan Army is, in theory, an Old Firm-free zone. Talking about wee teams like Brechin and Motherwell is allowed, as is the wearing of their jerseys. Celtic and Rangers, who dominate Scottish football for the rest of the year, are supposed to take a back seat. It is disappointing, therefore, to see fans in France sporting Celtic tops. Even more disappointing to hear a Rangers fan from a fishing village in north-east Scotland bring down the tone in a Paris bar by going on about his team. He is asked to desist and is now known as 'that Buchan Bluenose'.

Then, on this same day, I meet a Celtic fan and a Rangers supporter, who separately state that it is their first time away with Scotland. It will not be their last. In fact they have both decided not to follow the Old Firm teams to away matches. They will save their money for Scotland.

Wednesday, 10 June

Up and out early to Saint-Denis, the industrial suburb where the Scotland–Brazil game is being played. Tam Coyle, the wit and savant, has spotted on the town map that Saint-Denis has a street named after Bobby Sands, the Irish hunger striker. 'I'm away up the Rue Bobby Sands to see if I can buy a chicken supper,' says Tam. One of Tam's other routines is conversing with female England fans on the subject of goalkeepers. 'Do you prefer Seaman or Flowers?' he is wont to ask.

The atmosphere is strangely subdued in the town square. It is not helped by the fact that there is a raucous Radio 1 roadshow and the presenter has an excruciating English accent. There is a moment of light relief when Justin and friends of Del Amitri come onstage to do their Scotland France '98 song 'Don't Come Home Too Soon'. The debate is about to be settled on whether this official song or one of the many private enterprise alternatives best served the Scottish nation as an anthem for France '98.

Justin is getting on with a very nice acoustic version of his song when he has to stop. A dozen Scots in the front row have turned their backs and lifted their kilts. Whether their bare buttocks are a verdict on the song or a just a friendly greeting, Justin is laughing too much to continue. He does try but fails and eventually bursts into 'We're on the march with Ally's Army . . .'

• Time for a glass of France '98 champagne in a sunlit square before heading off to the Stade. Alex Salmond passes and at last I have met a celeb and even supplied the champagne. Alex says he is on his holidays, but you can see he is constantly being stopped by Scots fans for handshakes and photographs with babies. The SNP's rating in the polls is increasing by the minute.

• Outside the Stade I am overcome with anger, an emotion I had not anticipated experiencing on this long-awaited day. Ticketless Scots are offering huge sums of money to anyone with a spare brief. Meanwhile, there is a constant parade of FIFA fat cats into the stadium. The stewards have cordoned off a stretch of pavement to keep us common folk from getting in their way. This World Cup was preceded by dire warnings of the heavy penalties which would be meted out to any fans caught dealing in blackmarket tickets. Perhaps FIFA and the CFO, the French organising committee, might take some interest in the activities of a couple of chaps wearing Colombian accreditation badges who were spotted trying to flog tickets for £1,300 each.

• However, there were some successes for the ticketless ones. One Scots fan got in by deciding that if you can't beat the fat cats, you should join them. He simply tagged on to the end of a group of the suited ones and walked into the stadium. He explained the secret of his success: 'Wear a really smart suit so that you look the part. It also helps that I am quite continental in appearance.' Our man is a Scottish Asian and a very enterprising chap indeed.

• But not everyone in a suit was on the make. Beside me in the queue for the turnstile was a Raith Rovers fan who was still shell-shocked by the fact that he had managed to get a ticket. A kind Frenchman sold him a £133 ticket at face value and even gave him the change from 1,500 francs.

•The Stade de France is like a huge spaceship, and being there for the opening match was certainly something of an other-worldly experience. Trust the French to have a ceremony which featured 12-foot-tall dayglo orange insects and hundreds of little green men leaping about on the pitch. It was a strangely worrying sight after four days on the batter in Paris.

• Kick-off. It was all going so well at this World Cup until the football started. Things began to look ominous just after the opening ceremony when they put the goalposts up. Dangerous people around goals, these Brazilians. So it proved when a chap called Cesar stuck one in with the competition barely three minutes old. 'That will get Scotland angry,' said one fan hopefully.

They didn't get angry but they eventually got even through a penalty. As the Scottish fans prayed or reached for the heart pills, the penalty taker, John Collins, was the coolest man on the park. You could tell Mr Collins had the temperament for this match when he winked at the TV camera during the pre-match line-up.

It was half-time and Scotland were still in it, but the atmosphere was strangely muted. Apart from the Scottish fans who were being their usual magnificent, mental and barmy selves, the crowd appeared almost indifferent to the occasion. Many of the guests of the sponsors were obviously not fans. Football has come to a sad state when it is played in front of neutrals and invitees of the multinational companies.

Some of the fans of our fabled opponents were not much better. The received opinion is that the Brazilians are wonderful, happy, samba-swaying, cha-cha-chanting football fans. Perhaps I was unlucky with the Brazilians I was sitting near in the Stade, but they were a pretty morose bunch who only sang when they were winning and even then they didn't sing much. Even after Jim Leighton and Tom Boyd combined unwittingly to score Brazil's winning goal, they were not exactly cheery. They realised, as did the Tartan Army, that Brazil hadn't really beaten Scotland. Scotland had beaten themselves. Again.

• After the bitter experience of the Brazil match, there were words such as, 'We were not disgraced' and, 'At least our boys scored twice' and much more commonsense words as, 'Let's get the beers in'. There was, of course, the usual post-match ritual of peely-wally Scots trying to chat up dusky Brazilian babes. But you had to be careful. In a bar not too distant from the stadium, two Aberdeen fans were observing the ample charms of a bevy of Brazilians when an older and wiser companion advised them: 'Eyes aff, lads. They're loons.'

They were, indeed, examples of Brazil's major export to Paris, the transvestite. But the Tartan Army, as usual, had a song and a chant for the occasion: 'We're the famous Trannie Army, and we're here in gay Paree' and 'Get your balls out for the lads'. The balls, by the way, were two footballs which one of the Brazilians had in his/her otherwise empty bra.

• In another café in Saint-Denis there are a bunch of Scotland fans on a bus with a Glasgow travel firm who have every reason to be sombre. So far they have had two of their party run over, three mugged and one has 12 stitches in his head after a wee tumble. But what is grieving the lads most is the considerable amorous success one of their number is having with an English girl he has just met. In fact, she is busy consoling him in a corner of the café. The goings-on are of an extremely explicit nature. It is a case of Stand Up If You Love the English. While we are being explicit, it is as well to pass on the sighting of a kilted one who believes backsides painted with saltires have become passé. He has taken the art of body-painting form to new heights, or depths depending on your perspective. He has painted a face on what we have come to refer in Paris as his Eiffel. It was a wee smiling face and at least there was one part of one Scots fan that still had a cheery grin after that own goal.

• No number of pints, even at £5 each, could erase the vision in my mind – on a continuous loop – of Tommy Boyd scoring that own goal. David Quail of Glasgow put it in some perspective when he described the match against Brazil as 'Scotland updating our tragedy'.

Thursday, 11 June

Alasdair MacPhail was understandably miffed to read in *The Guardian* that the Tartan Navy was a Scottish myth. It was an 'outlandish' idea that a trawler-load of Scottish football fans would sail from Oban to Paris for the Brazil game. It was another romantic notion that would not come to pass.

Alasdair was reading this as he sat on the deck of his fishing boat, moored in the Seine just opposite the Eiffel Tower. Not only had Alasdair and his crew made it to Paris but they had navigated the Seine to within a mile of the Stade de France for the game.

They tied the boat to a no-parking sign. A Seine bateau-mouche turned up full of Brazilian VIPs. The Brazilians were bemused by the sight of the Scottish trawler bedecked in saltire flags and very much amused when Ian Munro, the kilted Fort William man with the wild beard, led them in a samba.

• The French media have a few more accurate reports on the Tartan Army. They were quite taken with the kilted Scots who were doing a Marilyn Monroe number with the updraught from a Metro ventilator near the Stade de France. *L'Equipe* put it rather nicely when they reported that the Scots were *'laissant apparaître leurs attributs de fiers Ecossais'*.

• For a group of people who spend so much time singing a ditty about Jimmy Hill which puts a negative spin on homosexuality, the Tartan Army appear quite happy to sleep in close proximity to their male friends. This could be misconstrued, as happened to two chaps in Paris. The small hotel room they shared had twin beds but pushed very close together.

It was the practice of the hotel every day to leave individually boxed chocolates on each bed. After a night of pre-match carousing one guy failed to return to the hotel until after breakfast time. His bed was left unslept in. That night the complimentary chocolates were found placed side by side on one bed. Paris is that kind of place.

•The economics of buying a beer on the Champs-Elysées can be daunting. The bears, of course, lug huge carry-outs of cheap supermarket beer wherever they go. The sophisticates fork out a fiver for a small glass from the cafés. There is another option.

Pop into McDonalds for a Maxi Meal. It consists of a Big Mac, a bag of chips and a drink of your choice. One of the options is beer. At £3.30, it is cheaper to buy the Maxi Meal, give the burger and chips away and drink the beer.

• The patience of the good people of the Rue François Miron has been stretched to breaking point. It is the location of the Auld Alliance bar and the street has been annexed by the Tartan Army. The entertainment involved a wee game of keepie-uppie. Inevitably, the ball ended up in a balcony.

Could they have their ball back? The problem was that no one was in. A friendly neighbour provided a ladder for the Scottish fan to climb up to fetch the ball. The fan was wearing his kilt, of course, and you are probably well aware by now what a Scots fan in a kilt does when he provided with a stage and an audience.

Ronnie Brown, the *patron* of the Auld Alliance, is humphy-backit carting in supplies of Tennent's lager, Irn Bru and various other Scottish delicacies. 'It's bad enough if we run out of Tennent's but we are in serious trouble if we have no Irn Bru for the morning after,' Ronnie said.

Ironically, the person to suffer a backlash from an Auld Alliance neighbour was not some loud-mouthed drunken kiltie but the estemed Radio Scotland presenter Ruth Wishart. Ruth had arranged to broadcast her Monday evening dinner-table chat show from the pub. But it was far too noisy, so Ronnie arranged for the recording to be done in the relative quiet of the back courtyard. It was at this point that a neighbour, whose open window looked on to the courtyard, exacted some revenge by playing music at full blast.

• Sad tales of carnage emerge from the Scottish invasion of Paris. Pipe Major Iain MacDonald tells me he was invited over to play the pipes at a sponsor's function. He was standing on a dais when he was grabbed in a bear-hug by an exiled Scot who found the experience all too moving. The free drink may also have been a factor. Inevitably, both fell over, with disastrous results for Iain. Three teeth knocked out but, much worse, the chanter of his much-valued bagpipes was snapped. 'They've been in the family for generations,' he said. 'They came unscathed through battlefields of the Boer War and two world wars and now they fail to survive a World Cup.'

• It is traditional for Scots to swap jerseys, scarves and hats with fans of other nations. Richard, from Glasgow, is regretting that he took the ritual a touch too far. In the heat of the celebrations on the Champs-Elysées, he was persuaded by a Brazilian chap to exchange his kilt for a pair of Hugo Boss breeks.

The plan was that the kilt would be returned the next day. Richard went to the George V hotel but both the Brazilian and the kilt, which had survived many World Cup trips, had gone.

• There was an unusual swap between Iain of Perth and Alison, a very comely American girl from Nashville who is studying in Paris. After having the significance of the ritual explained to her in terms of international goodwill, Alison agreed to the exchange. The blonde, blue-eyed all-American girl looked quite stunning in the navy-blue jersey. But not quite as eye-catching as Iain in his off-the-shoulder skinny-rib top.

Fashion note: the top was 100 per cent cotton from Victoria's Secret. The orange and red stripes did not really go with Iain's Black Watch tartan kilt.

• Wullie from Slough via Bellshill is quite the *roué* in his French beret. Dangling from his wrist is a ribbon attached to what used to be a balloon but is now a tattered bit of rubber. But Wullie is telling any French lady who will listen that it is his dog. It is a papillon, he tells them – the kind of fashionable dog you would have in Paris. Wullie actually has ladies feeding his dog lumps of sugar and bowls of water. As a reward for their generosity, Wullie gives them a kiss.

When not taking his dog for a walk, Wullie is yet another member of the Tartan Army sound-bite division. Wullie's latest gig was on German TV. Yes, he did mention the war.

• Some of the Tartan Army are in France without full planning permission from the wife. One chap, who shall remain nameless, knew there was no way he would be allowed to come to France. His wife said she would rip up his passport if he even suggested it. So he left the passport and his bag at his mate's house and stole into the night. When he finally phoned home to reveal his location, he was given 24 hours to return or his possessions would be in the street. He asked if she would be good enough to take his stuff down to his mum.

Friday, 12 June

The Tartan Army is moving on. We'll always have Paris, as Bogart said to Bergman in the film *Casablanca*. The Scots fans will have their memories, some hazier than others, of their World Cup visit to the city. For some considerable time too they will also have the Visa bills to remind them.

A Skye man (name withheld in case the bank manager is reading this) reports that his incidentals for the four days in Paris came to £2,000. Craig, an accountant from Perth, estimates that 10,000 spending an average of £1,000 means an injection of £10 million of Scottish money into an already overheated Parisian economy.

Even the bookies shop across the street charged £3 to get in for the privilege of losing more handfuls of francs.

With a full week between games and new cities to be discovered each time, the economics of France '98 became ever more daunting.

• Strathclyde polis have been keeping a discreet eye on the Scottish fans. Two of Glasgow's finest in plain clothes popped in to a bar on the Champs-Elysées to see how the Scots were getting on. Everything was just fine and not a tumbler broken until one of the cops turned to leave and knocked over a table laden with bottles and glasses. They exited the premises to friendly chants of 'Hooligans! Hooligans!'

• The Scots are perfectly capable of a bit of assault and robbery but this is only in the frantic pursuit of tickets for the match. A Scottish fan of Partick Thistle origin achieved his dream of getting into the Scotland–Brazil game by dint of a spot of thievery. He was having his picture taken by an Argentinian photographer. Having taken the snap, the photographer was rearranging the many cameras round his neck.

As he did so, he also took off his accreditation pass and left it on the ground. Yes, the Scot succumbed to temptation and such is the variable nature of the security here, that a 6ft 2ins fair-haired Scot in a kilt and a Brazil top and with no cameras managed to pass himself off as a 5ft 2ins Argentinian photographer.

Saturday, 13 June

Fans lucky enough to have any money left have made their way to Bordeaux to prepare for the match against Norway. The journey from Paris by TGV provided the opportunity for a spot of rest and recuperation and a chance to converse with football supporters of other nations. Danny from Glasgow found himself in conversation with an American.

The American and Danny had a lot in common, not least that they both work in the oil industry. Danny is a an electrician on the North Sea rigs. The American is vice-president of an oil company. The American said if Danny was ever looking for a job in the USA to contact him. Danny has a well-developed Scots sense of humour and was quite tickled to see from the business card that his new pal's name is Earl P. Champagne. So tickled, in fact, that he taken to calling himself Danny P. Lager.

• Bordeaux has done extremely well by the visiting fans. The stylish capital of claret country has created excellent tented villages with restaurants and bars offering good food and drink at reasonable prices. In the Café Mondial on the quayside you can quaff a glass of wine for £1 and watch all the World Cup action on a big screen.

• The above-mentioned Danny and his pals Steve and Drew have thrown themselves wholeheartedly into the Bordelaise dining experience, but not without the odd mishap. Steve thought he was ordering prawns but got snails; Drew wanted quail and ended up with mussels; and Danny, who thought he would keep it simple by ordering some ham, was confronted with a terrine in the shape of a frog attached to two genuine legs from the amphibious species.

• Scottish produce is very much to the fore in Bordeaux. Scotch lamb and Scotch whisky can be sampled in various eating establishments. The Scottish tent in the World Village has cans of Tennent's lager artistically displayed but tantalisingly unavailable in glass cabinets. Thankfully, the golden liquid from Glasgow can be had in the nearby Scottish beer tent.

The tent is run by the English owners of the Cambridge Arms in Bordeaux who are nice people but who severely underestimated the capacity of the Scottish supporters and have been routinely running out of supplies.

The Scottish complex, complete with official ceilidh bands and many unofficial bagpipers, has predictably become something of a centre of the action. So busy has it been that the Tartan Army have had to take over the Brazilian, Chilean, Spanish and French tents which had otherwise been lying empty of customers.

Many of Bordeaux's establishments have fallen to the Scots. In the Café Comedie, the patter is thick and fast. The Café Brun, it has been decided, is really named after Craig Broon.

A squad of Scots have even found a distillery for their post-match party tomorrow night. It is a giant bar called La Distillerie and the name above the door is Angus Dundee. There is unfortunately no eponymous Angus Dundee. In a conversation which I fear has lost much in the translation, the owner, Pierre Noujeim, explained the concept. It is named after the famous whisky The Dundee, he said, showing me a bottle.

The Dundee is a new brand to me and is produced by a Glasgow company called William Pitter Ltd. 'We are the only bar in Bordeaux to sell The Dundee,' Pierre said proudly. La Distillerie is a mixture of Pompidou Centre-style architecture and tartan wallpaper. It also features a very large-scale model of the working parts of a distillery. Drink can be purchased in big tubes which hold 2.5 litres of whatever liquid takes your fancy. The tubes are then inserted into a dispensing system on the table with a tap at each side. Just like any typical Scottish pub really; full of tubes.

The menu includes salmon, haggis and neeps, and Dundee cake. The Bordeaux smart set love the place. The visiting Scots appear bemused and not just with the drink. I have to report no great demand for the Dundee cake.

• The kilted ones are in good voice as usual but the song which they have most taken to does them little credit. It is about Ronaldo and has a rhyme about a cheeky smile and paedophile. My personal favourite is to the tune of 'Roamin' in the Gloamin'. It begins:
Reekin' in Brechin,
We were always steaming.
You were on the lager
And I was on the wine . . .
Unfortunately the lyrics then venture into territory unsuitable for reproduction for a genteel audience.

Sunday, 14 June
The contrast could not be more stark. While the English fans are engaged in bloody battles in Marseille, the Scots continue their party in Bordeaux.

It is midnight and Scottish Office Minister Brian Wilson, in Bordeaux for various trade and tourism promotions, is wandering through the crowds in the tented village in the centre of the city, chatting to fans and sharing a beer. Can you imagine the England fans giving such a friendly welcome to a politician and can you imagine an English Minister getting out among the supporters? Indeed, at this very moment, the *hooligans anglais*, as the French TV calls them, are head-butting and booting their way through the streets of Marseille.

The genial if boisterous and sometimes boorish behaviour of the Scots abroad has become something of a cliché. Journalists whose trade is tragedy and and the darker side of humanity despair of finding new ways to report that yet again the Tartan Army stretched the code of acceptable conduct to the limit and got away with it.

But the drunken kiltie is a much better motif for a nation than the sober skinhead whose idea of a good day is to put his boot into someone's face.

• Some Scots are going over the top. In fact, as Brian the Minister makes his way down the Allée de Tourny one fan, who has been celebrating rather too well in the Brazil tent, decides that the best place to be is on the roof. The structure appears able to support him as he sits on the roof drinking a bottle of wine by the neck, but the security staff tell him they would much rather he continued his celebrations on the ground. One of the security men holds the fan's bottle of wine while the other helps him down. The bottle is returned, the fan shakes the security staff by the hand, thanks them for their consideration and rejoins the party inside the tent.

• It is not all noise and stramash down here in claret country. There are a number of very swish events to be attended on the reader's behalf. Brian the Minister absolutely insisted that we attend a reception at Saint-Lambert. This is not a canonisation of the Scotish midfielder. It is the location of Château Malecot, a winery in Pauillac. The château is the home of the Johnston family who came from Scotland to Bordeaux in 1720 to make their fortune in the wine trade.

We agreed to go to this event, sip claret and malt whiskies and graze on top-notch canapés because Brian the Minister explained that it is essential Scotland uses its World Cup profile to promote our produce since the ultimate end product of this is jobs back home.

Jean-Marie Johnston, present head of this claret clan, treats us to Auld Alliance, a blend of wine he has made especially for the Scots. In his short speech, Jean-Marie says he is amazed at how much wine is shipped to Scotland, a small nation of five million people. In his brief reply, Brian the Minster says that Greenock might be a factor in this.

Brian presents Jean-Marie with a bottle of 17-year-old Bowmore malt and in return receives a bottle of 1982 Grand Duroc Millon which he is looking forward to drinking once he has ascertained that its value does not exceed the £160 value set down by protocol. Early indications from sources within the wine trade are that The Minister is okay on this one.

As the Auld Alliance warms up, Davie, a fish merchant from Aberdeen, just happens to have with him his banjo, Martin from Bordeaux via Perth has his guitar and Jean-Marie, the drop-dead elegant Franco-Scot produces his moothie. In the delightful setting of the lobby of the château, the French and Scots have a wee ceilidh to themselves.

• It transpires that the above-mentioned Davie from Aberdeen is a member of another Tartan Navy. They have sailed a converted lifeboat from Lowestoft in southern England to Cherbourg on the northern coast of France. On the way they nearly collided with a channel ferry. The skipper of their crew is a chap called Doddie. At every available opportunity, Davie gives a rendition of 'It's a long way with Doddie's Navy'. It may or may not be a long way from Lowestoft to France but it is certainly a lot further from Oban whence our man Alasdair MacPhail sailed.

• The Scots fans are in France to make love not war. (Only the single and unattached supporters that is.) Some are more blatant than others, like the chap who has on the back of his Scotland top where the name should be the words 'J'adore'. His squad number is 69. An American girl attracts more than a bit of attention in the tented village with her T-shirt which had the word 'Shag' on the front. She was at pains to point out that in the USA this word means to dance.

Monday, 15 June

The people of Bordeaux have woken up to the television and newspaper reports of the appalling scenes involving the *hooligans anglais* in Marseille. They are beginning to appreciate having the Scots and Norwegians in their town. The Scots are noisy. They leave more than the odd broken bottle in the street. They urinate in the nice pot plants in the tented vilage in the Allee de Tourny. But then so do some of the locals. One Scot decides to shake hands with a fellow pisseur as they stand at opposite sides of a pot plant. 'Hands across the water,' he says.

The Norwegians do not make nearly so much noise, break fewer bottles and are just happy to be in a place where the drink is so cheap. They are an amiable bunch and merely smile when the Scots chant at them: 'Sing when you're whaling, you only sing when you're whaling.' The Bordeaux people, who had kept a wary distance from the kilted ones and the vikings, begin to join in the party.

• Another day, another château. Today it is the famous Château Lascombes where the gentlepersons of the Scottish media have been invited for a visit by Tennent's, the lager people, who have an interest in the place. We are gathered around a swimming-pool sipping the Lascombes rosé before embarking on an inspection of the winery.

The wine is going down nicely but my glass is empty. I spy a full bottle of the delicious chilled stuff and reach out for it. Just as I do so, there is a blur of movement and Charlie Nicholas, late of Celtic and now with as many media jobs as Dougie Donnelly, has got in first. 'I always was very quick over the last ten yards,' Charlie says. But at least he does pour me a glass.

• There is a dinner at the city hall where Bordeaux's mayor is entertaining Brian Wilson and other Scots. I really should be there to report the goings-on of the great and good. But I have been waylaid in the tented village by Ian Adie and the rest of the Wee-ist Pipe Band in the World. The band has a trailer-load of Tennent's lager which we must get through. Dinner consists of a chip baguette which the Scots have now introduced as a local delicacy.

The Wee-ist Pipe Band and sundry other pipes and drums lead a parade of at least 5,000 Scots and quite a few Norwegians through the city centre. It is riotous and at the same time controlled. Old ladies out for their evening stroll are courteously conducted through the crowds, their hands kissed respectfully. Younger women are urged to join the procession and kissed more enthusiastcally. One of the songs is: 'We're nice and we know we are . . .'

Tony Banks, the English Sports Minister, has got it right for once. The Tartan Army is behaving itself to spite the English. Bordeaux is stunned by the scenes. Bordeaux is smiling.

• Brian, the Minister allocated the Bordeaux shift, has been assiduous in his official duties promoting Scotland and mingling with the fans. He was approached by one Scot who gave him an especially warm welcome. Why was the chap so pleased to see The Minister, as we have come to call Mr Wilson? He was a constituent and The Minister had helped him get a house in Dalry seven years ago.

• Part of The Minister's packed schedule involved visiting local travel agents to promote holidays in Scotland. There was a slight organisational hiccup at one agency. The Minister and his minders were ushered into seats. The owner came out and asked where it was they would like to book their holiday.

• The bad news about missing that official dinner is that there were match tickets to be had if you made the right contacts.

The Minister met a high-ranking French official who said that a few tickets had become available at the last minute and could The Minister find a good home for them? Brian thought he very well might be able to.

Thus two decent young men, still sober at 1 a.m. on this night before the match, who had approached The Minister on the very subject of spare tickets struck lucky. From being members of the great ticketless hordes they were elevated to VIP status with a glass of champagne before the game and seats in front of Jim Farry.

• Never has singing for your supper been more successful than the little number performed at the dinner by film-maker Peter Broughan. Peter is a fair chanter and is not one to let an occasion go by without an appropriate song.

Peter was still ticketless the night before the match, but was making the most of life by attending the official dinner laid on by the mayor for Scottish dignitaries. As a tribute to his hosts and in honour of France, Peter give a storming rendition of 'The Marseillaise'. Having studied French at a good Tim school in Glasgow, he knew the words by heart.

So moved was one of the French hosts that he insisted Peter join him for the match with one condition – that he was allowed to borrow Peter's kilt for the occasion.

Tuesday, 16 June

Scottish fans can be cruel. There I was dressed for the sunshine on this day of the Scotland–Norway match. To cope with the heat I had to resort to the tailored green tartan shorts and the panama hat purchased at Marks & Spencer for this eventuality. Okay, words like chic and panache did not come into it, but my erstwhile chum on the trip, Daniel P. Lager (see previous reports for details), cut to the quick with his greeting: 'Hello, Tam. I see you're out for your Hallowe'en.'

• In the champagne tent in the Allée de Tourny the more upmarket fans gather for the pre-match warm-up. There is a definite feeling that some were preparing for the traditional role of being magnanimous and cheerful in defeat. How else can you explain a pre-match chant of 'We're shite but we drink champagne'?

• The Scots have come from all over the world to be at Bordeaux. There are badges and flags of such as the Abu Dhabi Tartan Army, the Hong Kong Tartan Army and the New York East Village Tartan Army.

We also have the makings of a Japanese Tartan Army. He is called Tadake from Tokyo. He is over in France following his own team but has enlisted with the Scots. You can tell by the astonishment on his face and the bemused grin as he surveys the scenes that he has never seen anything quite like it. He wears a Scotland top under his Japan jersey. He has a saltire painted on his cheek and sports the Jimmy hat. The kilt, he says, is next on the shopping list.

• Those who search for omens can find one on a flagpole on an office building in the Allée. The flagpole is vacant and Ian from Newbury via Perth, who specialises in getting Scottish *drapeaux* in place, gives the residents a Lion Rampant and persuades them to put it up. Unfortunately, being French and therefore not very good at organising anything, the residents put the Lion Rampant upside down and at half-mast. Ian, not a man to tempt fate, shows them how to get it right.

• Match time approaches and fans on their way to the Stade Lescure on the free public transport laid on by the city of Bordeaux are susprised to see someone remarkably like Ally McCoist standing on the pavement trying in vain to hail a taxi. It is indeed Super Ally, late as usual for his urgent TV appointment at the game.

Stewart, a Scots supporter over from Western Australia, persuades the driver to stop the bus and Ally is hailed aboard. In return, Stewart asks Ally to record a quick video message for his mum Rita who is a big fan. The Scotland No 9, who is not exactly camera-shy, readily agrees.

• What a difference a goal makes. This scribe of little faith was set to head off early and write the France '98 obituary for Scotland. Flo had scored against the flow for Norway and Scotland were heading once more for the category of gallant losers.

I was beginning to think that the chap had it right who had consumed quite a lot of his five-litre plastic container of Vin de Pays de Pyrénées Orientales and was now asleep using the container as a pillow.

Then Burley equalised and tumult broke out. My pint of Kronenbourg was sent sky-high. Luckily I was hit on the head with a bottle – luckily because the bottle was plastic and contained a decent quantity of red wine with which to celebrate Scotland's continued presence in the World Cup with the best fans in the world.

You will gather that my view of the Scotland–Norway match was not from the stands with the fat cats in the Stade Lescure. I was with the *sans culottes*, the ticketless ones, who were watching the game in the Café Mondial, a tented village with a giant screen on the Bordeaux quayside.

Bathed in glorious sunshine and just delirious to be in the vicinity of the action, the Scots had a little ditty for the CFO, the French World Cup organising committee. We will not give chapter and verse but it suggested a certain *trou* into which they could insert their tickets.

There are many worse places to watch a game of football than the Café Mondial. There was much to be had of the glorious, locally produced claret. Scotland fans, used to a basic football diet of pies, were dining at half-time on steak and chips. Some Scots, obviously pining for the simpler food of home, were educating the chefs in the Café Mondial restaurants in the creation of the baguette filled not with ham or cheese but with chips.

Scotland outnumbered Norway in the Café Mondial by a thousand to one. On the banks of the Garonne we sang 'The Bonnie, Bonnie Banks of Loch Lomond'. The Norwegians were silent and the Scots chanted that they 'only sing while they're whaling'.

The Scots have something to celebrate and so do the Norwegians and they party together. In a restaurant in old Bordeaux town, I find Wullie from Slough via Bellshill. He was last seen in Paris using an empty dog leash and collar as a prop to engage in conversation with locals. Wullie and his cohorts now have T-shirts with a photo of a canine and the words: *Où est le dug?* One lady has actually offered to accompany them to the police station to report their loss.

The restaurant is full of Norwegians. Le Dug team rearrange all the seats into a single row. As the mystified Norwegians sit down in a line, Wullie leads the singing, complete with actions, to the tune of 'Michael Row the Boat Ashore'. The new words are: 'Vikings row the boat ashore, hallelujah . . .'

The Norwegians soon get into the swing of things and the restaurant becomes a longship, complete with a lashing from Wullie for the galley slaves. The Norwegian comprehension disappears when Le Dug team burst into: 'The back of the boat they cannae sing.'

Also spotted in celebratory mode in a café is a former Celtic player and coach. For some unaccountable reason a chant of 'Stand up if you hate Jock Brown . . .' begins. First on his feet is Murdo McLeod, victim of the end-of-season fall-out at Celtic Park.

In the Café Brun, Danny P. Lager and company have been such good customers that *le patron*, or Jimmy Five Bellies as they have christened him, has ordered his barman Jean-Pierre, or Ginola as they have named him, to crack open a bottle of Taittinger for the lads.

The Scots are singing 'We're gonna qualify . . .' Who's that standing just inside the doorway. It's The Minister and he's joining in.

Wednesday, 17 June

Such was the extent and volume of the singing after the match that many fans have woken up with sore throats which give a whole new meaning to croak monsieur.

The Tartan Army wake up to find that Bordeaux loves them. *'Ils nous manquent deja!'* is the headline in Sud-Ouest, the local newspaper, 'Missing you already!' It illustrates the extremely good time the Scots, the Norwegians and the Bordelais have had over the last few days with a game of football as the excuse.

Reporter Benoit Lasserre enthuses: *'Bordeaux, ville anglaise? La bonne blague! Bordeaux, ville écossaise!'* A town which had a reputation for its English ways had been won over by the Scots.

Words like *'gentillesse'* and *'courtoisie'* can be pasted into the Tartan Army scrapbook along with *'sens de la fête'* and *'l'amitié'*. There may have been a few broken beer bottles on the pavements, he says, but let's not spoil memories of a great party with such quibbles.

You might be forgiven for thinking that M. Lasserre had been on a beer or two himself with a paragraph of purple and impenetrable prose which mentioned both the water of Loch Ness and the prohibition police work of Eliot Ness. His conclusion was more straightforward: *'Ne me kilt pas!'* A plea to the kilted ones to stay, please stay.

• Cammy from Fife has financed his trip to this costly tournament by the simple expedient of selling his house. This statement is quite a conversation stopper even among the ranks of the fanatical kilted ones. But Cammy has a rational explanation. He is a single man so it's not as if he's putting wife and weans on the homeless list. 'I can always buy another house but there will never be another 1998 World Cup.'

As Cammy related this in the alley of fun which the Allée de Tourny has become, he had more pressing problems. The combination of heat and chafing under his kilt meant certain dangly spherical objects under his kilt were 'on fire'. Requests to various French girls to borrow some cream ('but nae scented', Cammy stipulated) were unsuccessful. A Scotswoman, a nurse on her hols but still in Florence Nightingale mode, was able to supply some ultimately soothing Germolene. 'Could you put the cream on for me,' Cammy asks. 'Sorry, you're not in BUPA' is the reply.

• I must have passed the Grande Théâtre in Bordeaux a dozen times in the last few days, but it took an e-mail from Cecilia in the West End of Glasgow to tell me about a wee incident there. The steps of the Grande Théâtre provided a natural amphitheatre for celebrating Scottish fans. The trouble was that the doors were due to open for an evening performance and the front-of-house staff were concerned about the audience gaining access.

Susan Capdequi, a Glaswegian living in Bordeaux and working at the theatre, was deputed to sort things out. Somewhat nervously she approached a kilted one and explained the problem. 'Nae problem, hen,' he said and shouted: 'Come on, lads, the lady wants us tae move.' With that the battalion moved off as one.

'More brownie points for the Tartan Army and increased promotion prospects for Susan,' says Cecilia.

• One company which declined to participate in the Scots products promotion in Bordeaux was Barr's Irn Bru, they apparently want their product to be perceived as an international and not just a Scottish brand. They have nevertheless received constant publicity, as many have taken to the Dario G France '98 anthem to which have been added the words 'Irn Bru! Irn Bru!' Unlike in Paris, supplies of Irn Bru have been almost impossible to come by in Bordeaux.

It has been available only as part of the Scottish survival kit being handed out by the *Daily Record* tartan bus which is travelling around France with the fans. In charge of *The Record* bus is one Bob Shields, the journalistic black sheep of the family who has finally come in useful.

• Much fun has been had by well-heeled Scottish supporters who managed to wangle invitations to the many wine-producing châteaux in the Bordeaux area. The hospitality has been unstinting. One group who had drunk well but not too wisely, decided that a carry-out would be in order. They dropped a few bottles of wine out of the window to be collected on the way to minibus which would take them back to their hotel.

Unfortunately, the owner of the château had chosen this moment to take some air and they were caught claret-handed. Being a Frenchman of impeccable manners he said nothing but collected the errant bottles and handed them to the Scots as a *petit cadeau*.

• Amidst the cheers and celebrations at the Stade Lescure, there was a poignant moment. As the game ended, a couple who had been sitting quietly, laid a bouquet of flowers and a saltire with the name Gerard on a seat that should have been occupied but sadly wasn't.

• With a week between games, fans are faced with difficult choices of where and how to spend the intervening days. Not a few Scots are prolonging their stay in this city with which they have struck up a *nouvelle* alliance.

In the world village in the Allée de Tourny they are hanging on for a last tango in the Argentinian tent, a final samba in Café Bresil and a farewell scoop of Tennent's lager in the Scottish pub. The Bordelais are now turning up in increasingly large numbers to observe the flickering flames of the Scottish party. So *cordiale* is the *entente* that fans are finding free drinks and food put their way by local establishments who have done well financially from the tartan invasion, but who also want to express the town's thanks for a memorable experience.

• My last word from a local comes from Pierre-Yves Squiggle (sorry, I can't make out his last name in my notebook.). 'For Bordeaux the World Cup is over. It will not be the same without

Scotland,' he said quite late on in the Café Brun. Pierre-Yves is very emotional. So he should be. He has been out partying with the Scots for four days.

Thursday, 18 June

I moved on from Bordeaux to Toulouse where there was a different attitude towards football fans.

Toulouse prides itself on being the most welcoming city in France. Being so close to Spain, Toulouse is no stranger to the fiesta. This weekend was to be special. The national Fête de la Musique coincided with the city's annual cavalcade and a programme of World Cup events.

But the party is off. *Les hooligans anglais* have rained on Toulouse's parade. M. La Tournerie, the chief of police, has decreed that the city battens down the hatches in anticipation of the English.

Innocent victims of the curfew are Danish and South Africans in town for their match and the Toulousians who are unable to celebrate their national team's 4–0 victory over Saudi Arabia and qualification for the next round.

'*C'est une ville morte*,' says Christian Esgrine, *patron* of Le Paddy bar and restaurant. Christian called his bar Le Paddy because of the whisky which gives him such a hangover when he goes on hunting holidays in Ireland. There must be some Irish blood as well as Irish whiskey in Christian's veins. He has organised a wee lock-in for a few fans after the officially ordained closing time of 11 p.m. The bars in Toulouse normally stay open until 2 a.m. or 3 a.m. When there is a fiesta some of them don't close at all.

A dozen or so Danish fans, as well as a few Scots and French conga around Le Paddy in defiance of the prevailing gloom. It was a slight flavour of what might have been.

• Such is the reputation of the English fans, that Carsten Andersen, a banker from Copenhagen, and his friends, decided to spend as little time as possible in Toulouse. They drove 1,200 miles from Copenhagen for the South Africa game. Instead of risking a confrontation with *les hooligans*, they drove the extra 150 miles across the Spanish border to spend the night in Barcelona. 'Reports on Danish TV made anywhere with English supporters sound like a war zone,' he says.

Even English fans were baling out of Toulouse four days ahead of their country's match against Romania. A young Liverpudlian who did not want to be named said: 'We haven't any tickets. We came to France for the atmosphere, but who wants to be around this kind of atmosphere?'

Derek, a Yorkshireman, is in France selling flags, scarves and hats to supporters of all countries. He is also over to enjoy himself. 'I was working selling my stuff at the Scotland–Norway match in Bordeaux and then I stayed up all night. It was a great party. But I'll be keeping my distance from the English.'

• The Toulouse press has been vociferous in its criticism of *les anglais*. *La Dépêche* quotes Gegene, owner of the Trois Petits Cochons bar, as saying: 'These Huns are holding our city hostage. They have kidnapped our trade.'

A vitriolic opinion article describes *les anglais* as 'vile and ignorant monsters' with little trace of brain activity and an average vocabulary of 3.2 words. There are many and varied other insults beyond the ken of our small Collins French dictionary and the translating powers of the nice lady receptionist at the Hotel les Beaux Arts.

• One of the treats laid on by Toulouse for visiting fans is a free boat trip on the river Garonne from the city centre to the stadium, which is built on an island. Scores of Scotland fans had come to see the Denmark–South Africa match. As they sailed up river in the company of Danish, French, Jamaican and decent England fans, the Scots treated them to a rendition of 'We are sailing . . .'. You can't keep a good fan down.

• Like most host cities, Toulouse has put up a tented village to offer refreshment and entertainment to visiting fans. Local traders have invested heavily in stands at the Village Occitan on the banks of the Garonne near the stadium. You can buy anything from armagnac to automobiles from the stalls.

There is a big screen – which should have shown the match for those unable to get tickets – but it was switched off on the orders of M. la Tournerie, chief of police. The bars and restaurants in the village lay virtually empty. It was a football village with no football.

Traders chafed and complained about lost revenue. Supporters headed off to find a bar with a TV. Meanwhile, there was only one TV working in the village, the one in the police tent where the officers who might usefully have been supervising events at the big screen were watching the game.

• The promises of the French organisers about cracking down on ticket touts have proved to be emptier than the Toulouse football village on match day. English touts practised their dodgy trade openly in front of police at the security barricades at the Stade Municipal.

One particularly foul-mouthed Cockney was berating Danish fans who expressed doubts about the validity of his tickets. The tout dragged one Dane up to a policeman and shouted: 'Tell this f****** idiot that these tickets are okay.' The policeman remained aloof, as the French polis do.

A French ticket tout nearby was attempting to fleece fans with a bunch of tickets for last week's game concealed under one genuine brief. It seems the touts and charlatans, as well as the hooligans, are being given *carte blanche* to ruin this tournament.

• France '98 is a truly international experience. Malcom Mac-donald is a lucky man in that he has dual nationality. Malcolm was born in Edinburgh but was brought up in Edenvale, South Africa.

He was at the Scotland games in Paris and Bordeaux in the kilt and dark-blue jersey of his native land. He attends the South African games in the bright colours of his adopted country.

Malcolm was made redundant recently from his job as an insurance manager. He is spending large chunks of his redundo on a five-week trip with his mates which takes in all of the World Cup and the Test match cricket in England.

If Scotland had got to meet South Africa, which they didn't, Malcolm would have been the guy in the kilt and the South Africa top cheering both teams.

• A postscript to Bordeaux. Jimmy and Eddie, *The Diary*'s chums at Passport Travel in Clydebank, tell us they were concerned about the treatment their clients might receive at Bordeaux airport in the light of the bad publicity generated by *les anglais*. They contacted Jean-Bernard Landeche, the airport director, asking him not to confuse the Scots and the English and requesting that he did not close the refreshment facilities and duty-free shops.

M. Landeche replied: 'We have already noted in Bordeaux that Scottish supporters have a different view of enjoying themselves. They were colourful, very noisy but nice people and charming with French women. Our caféteria, bars, restaurants, all shops and duty-free will be wide open tonight at the airport for your supporters. I hope Scotland qualify for the second run.'

Friday, 19 June

South to the small town of St-Rémy-de-Provence where the Scotland squad have their training camp. The whole town is swathed in saltires. Craig Brown's tactic of winning the hearts and minds of the local population has worked. In fact there is a mutual Scottish–Provencale love affair going on.

By chance, I arrive in the town square in the middle of a party for the team and the people of St-Rémy. The team in kilts, white shirts, and ties are sitting on the steps of the town hall. They are being serenaded by St-Rémy schoolchildren. They are singing 'Flower of Scotland' and when they get to the bit about 'your wee bit heel and glen' it is uplifting and poignant. Brings a tear to a glass eye as us cynics would say.

The mayor, M. Herve Cherubini, makes a speech about the new alliance between Provence and Scotland. On the subject of the team's chances, he says: 'We are confident we can make it through to the second round.' Like most people in St-Rémy he is now a true dark blue. Jack McGinn replies in his best schoolboy French and does reasonably well. We will forgive him the pronunciation of aussi which made it sound as if there was an Australian contingent present.

At the free bar there is a choice of bottles of McEwan's Wee Heavy beer or Ricard. To celebrate the alliances, auld and new, it seems appropriate to have a hauf and hauf of both. And very potent it is too.

• The party in the square provides the first France '98 encounter with Gerry Brady. Gerry is a Dundee United and Scotland fan whose dedication to following Scotland is matched only by his insistence that it must all be in style and usually to excess. I had hoped to meet up with Gerry in Bordeaux, if only to see the digs that he had organised.

Through a friendly priest in Dundee, Gerry had sourced a

monastery in Saint-Emilion which could offer cheap but classy accommodation. When he turned up, Gerry discovered that he was more than welcome but the monastery had just entered a fortnight-long period of retreat during which total silence had to be observed. Deciding that this ambience would not be great for the crack, Brady and company decamped to the delights of a nearby petit château which took in paying guests.

Predictably, when I said to Gerry that I was off to find a modest pension, he would have none of it. He had taken rooms in a country house on the outskirts of town and nothing would have it but our party should book in as well.

So it was a quiet Saturday night in St-Rémy. Apart from the dinner for 12. Apart from the singing. Apart from the conga into which were incorporated sundry American and other nationalities of tourists.

Home and so to bed. Well, not quite. The country house had a magnificent swimming-pool and a huge lawn set in a lavender garden. It was a starry, starry night in Provence. A wee dip in the shallow end of the pool. Then a glass of wine by Baron Philippe Rothschild in a setting by Vincent Van Gogh. It is not a bad place to be and it will certainly do until we find somewhere better.

Saturday, 20 June
Time to relax and take a walk around St-Rémy. It is the second time I have been here. The last time was in September 1985, 11 September 1985 to be precise. I remember the date as I walk past the shop where I bought a French newspaper that day. I walk into the shaded courtyard of the hotel where I remember turning to the sports pages of the French newspaper hoping to find a report on the Wales–Scotland qualifying match for the Mexico 1986 World Cup. I remember reading a headline with the words Stein and *mort*. I remember the shock and then the hope that *mort* was some kind of metaphor for a defeat, a reversal echoing Bill Shankly's phrase about football being more important than life or death.

Scotland had not been defeated. They had won through to the next round of the World Cup but had lost Jock Stein. Sitting in the shaded courtyard some 13 years later I thought of Jock Stein but more painfully of the people I have lost since then.

Sunday, 21 June
Scotland fans are gathering in Saint-Etienne for what is the end of

the beginning but hopefully not the beginning of the end of their France '98 campaign. Tired, sunburnt, severely bruised in the wallet and suffering meltdown of the credit-card plastic, the supporters are preparing for the confrontation with Morocco.

After cosmopolitan Paris and sophisticated Bordeaux, the Scots are on the receiving end of a down-to-earth but warm welcome from post-industrial Saint-Etienne. A full programme of events has been laid on to occupy the fans in the days and hours before the match tomorrow. Some of these, it has to be said, have left the visitors slightly puzzled.

There is to be a Café Litteraire at which readings will be delivered and speeches made on the subject of football and literature. Indeed the mayor of Saint-Etienne himself, M. Michel Thiolliere, who is a bit of a writer, will make one of the speeches. He is a brave man since his contribution will be made in Le Glasgow, one of the more popular bars in town, just three hours before kick-off.

Fifty Gaels have made their way from Point on the Isle of Lewis to Saint-Etienne to take part with 50 Moroccans in a cultural exchange. Children in schools and community centres are learning Gaelic songs and Highland dancing. There is also a story-telling competition between the Gaels and the Moroccans. We are not sure of the rules of engagement of this particular contest but our money is on the people from Point.

• The Scots fans don't ask for much when it comes to facilities, so a small park in the centre of Saint-Etienne fills the bill more than adequately. It has a tent which serves kebabs, chips and cold beer.

There is an egregious fountain with a large pool in which the fans can disport themselves. The aqua aerobics are not merely showing off. It is more than 100 degrees here (even Mexicans are being admitted to hospital with heatstroke) and the fountain provides some relief. The park also forms a natural amphitheatre in which the Stephanois, the inhabitants of Saint-Etienne, can watch the ritual of the celebrating Scots. It makes a change from another quiet Sunday. Each song gets a ringing round of applause and, as you might guess, this is encouraging the Tartan Army to come out of their shells.

Observing one very wet young Scotsman walk along the main street leaving bloody footprints, prompts us to give the following advice. Don't break beer bottles in the fountain before you go paddling therein.

• When Scots fans finally grabbed some sleep it can be in unusual locations. Bus shelters, carparks and park benches are quite normal. Mark, a fish trader from Arran, set a new standard by spending the night in a volcano. He got separated, as you do, from his chums on the journey from Bordeaux to Saint-Etienne.

He fell into the company of some mushroom pickers and gypsies, as you normally don't. It was the gypsies who suggested to Mark that he take refuge for the night in the volcano near Clermont-Ferrand. They even provided him with a sheet.

• A comely blonde is the only female on a bus-load of Tartan Army bears making their way around France '98. Being a low-budget operation, it is necessary for her to share a room. She has picked on a youngish chap who is rather handsome. Not because she is hoping for any romantic interludes. She based her choice purely on the fact that her room-mate never gets back to the hotel before noon and even then only for a quick shower.

• Alastair Murray of Glasgow sent an e-mail with a tale of woe about the Brazil–Scotland opening game. He is currently working in Kazakhstan but was determined that he would be at the match. His work schedule meant that he was due to return home on 10 June, the day of the big game. Being of an optimistic stripe, he used his trusty Amex card to buy two tickets and book the relevant flights to Paris.

So tight was the schedule that he could not be certain whether he would even be in the Stade de France for the kick-off. The plan was that his beloved Andrena would make her way from Glasgow to Paris, leaving his match ticket at Stansted airport. Everything went very well. He left on the morning of the tenth, driving for three hours from Aksai to Uralsk to catch the five-hour flight to Stansted, arriving at Stansted in time for his flight to Paris.

He went to the KLM/UK desk to secure the tickets left by his girlfriend when she had passed through on her way to Paris that morning. One slight problem was that no-one at the airline desk knew anything about any envelope with the precious World Cup tickets. A search failed to produce any sign of it and the flight to Paris was due to depart. A despondent Mr Murray decided that there was no point in going to Paris without a ticket.

He headed home to Glasgow where he was woken about midnight by a phone call from Andrena. She had not had a good day either. As she sat in the Stade and the game wore on, she realised that Alastair wasn't going to make it to the match.

She placed his Scotland top on the empty seat and proceeded to look generally forlorn. A feeling that was not improved when she had to explain to puzzled Scots sitting beside her that her man had failed to turn up. 'This is some place to get chucked by your boyfriend,' one of them said sympathetically.

• In Saint-Etienne I receive an e-mail from Hong Kong about the high jinks of a Dundee girl now living in Paris. Global stuff, or what. Laura Fisher is on to tell us of the Clootie City exile who was so delighted to find herself surrounded by her countrymen in her own wee Paris local that she decided to perform her own version of the Highland Fling in their honour. The result of her over-energetic jigging was a sprained ankle.

She ended up on crutches. Working, as she does, in a city which is *trés* snob, she could not admit that her injury was the result of football celebration. She told colleagues she was hurt at her karate class.

• Also on the injury front, there are many sore heads on this trip. One group of fans diverted themselves by sitting in a café sipping water and translating from the French the instructions on the packet of pain-killers just purchased by one of their number. 'You should be fine now,' one said, 'this medicine is for painful periods.'

• Finally on the injury front, is the chap with a mini-stookie on his pinkie and a fortuitous two-week line which has allowed him to come to France '98. What happened, big man? 'Oh, I hit it with a hammer.'

Monday, 22 June

Those whose business it is to report blood and snotters at this World Cup forecast that Saint-Etienne with its large Arab population would be be the flashpoint as Scotland plays Morocco. There was a hint on the first few days that this might be the case as the then small numbers of the Tartan Army were confronted by Moroccan youths who were interested in swapping semiotic insults. The Scots diplomatically refused to become involved.

The insults have now stopped, either because there are many thousands of kilted ones in town and there is power in numbers or, a preferred option, that the Moroccans have decided it is better to join in the fun.

• The bourgeoisie of Saint-Etienne are most certainly behind the Scots partly, alas, for racist reasons. But the decision by well-off Stephanois to accommodate Scottish fans on a B&B basis has not been taken for economic reasons. Visitors paying only £20 a night are being fed, watered and chauffeured to and from the city centre by locals who just want to extend a warm welcome.

Gary, Craig and the other Gary from Glasgow have landed on their feet digs-wise. Like a few other Scots, they have been down to the florist to order bouquets of flowers as a gesture of appreciation for their landlady. The arrival of the flowers coincide with a stressful few hours for their landlady. Her wee dog has got lost but it is eventually found. Shortly after the dog is returned, the florist delivers the flowers. She is in floods of tears.

• The Stephanois are keen to learn about the Scottish culture which is on show here. As yet another choral performance is put on in a fountain, a local asks: 'What are they singing about?' The Scots are doing their Irn Bru chant. 'They are singing about a popular boisson, a soft drink, which is much favoured by Scots who have a *guele de bois*, a hangover,' I reply. There is something of a gap of understanding on this one.

• I find Cammy of Fife, the man who sold his house to come to the World Cup, with many sprigs of heather in front of the town hall. The sprigs are part of his efforts to defray the heavy costs of France '98. Before surrendering the keys to his house, Cammy harvested his entire heather garden and made a large quantity of sprigs. He sold 200 in Paris and Bordeaux and has 150. The travel and hot weather has taken its toll on the unsold sprigs. Cammy has had to treat them with hairspray to prevent the heather bells falling off.

• The Scots are still bemused by the prices in France. One group of fans, eking out their remaining francs, remonstrated with *le patron* of a small *estaminet*. They thought that 1045 francs, about

£105, was pretty steep for six beers and one pizza. Le *patron* agreed and pointed out that the 1045 was in fact 10.45 p.m., the time their bill had been issued.

• Money may be tight but the chaps are not starving at the camp-site in Saint-Etienne. Some concrete blocks were liberated and put to use as the base for a barbecue. Acorns, pine cones and bits of wood were collected as fuel. The problem of a grill upon which to cook their steaks was solved by the temporary purloining of a drain cover.

• It looked as if the World Cup was over after the first game for one Glasgow fan. He had frittered away his entire budget in the fleshpots of Paris. He was in gloomy mode having a last beer and saying farewell before setting off for home when another Scottish fan took him aside and gave him £500 which could be paid back 'whenever'. The benefactor explained that he had made quite a bit of money selling wacky baccy to the various football fans in France. Even our drug-dealers are nice.

• Despite early fears of difficulties between Scotland fans and Moroccan immigrants, reports are coming in of fraternisation. The scene is a small bar in the Arab quarter. Three Glasgow boys are buying drinks for their new Moroccan chums. The Moroccans are not really into alcohol and reciprocate with plates of chips and kebabs. When it was time for the Moroccans to stand a round again, one of them says he couldn't possibly have another drink but would the lads like to sample some very fine hashish.

• After two week's immersion, Scots are becoming much more fluent in French. New phrases include *Le petit chat est frappé sur la tête* (The kitty's deid) and *Qui est sur le ding-dong?* (Who's on the bell?)

• The plan was to have a quiet night to prepare for tomorrow's decisive game against Morocco. The plan is ruined by the English. They do so by losing 2-1 to Romania. The Tartan Army watching the game on the big screen in the square had turned Romanian for the occasion, with hand on heart as their national anthem was sung. The Scots countered 'God Save the Queen' with 'Flower of

Scotland'. They even sang 'The Marseillaise' for the French referee.

Petrescu scored the winning goal and the Romanians sent the English home to think again.

All this and the £15 set-dinner menu in Les Colonnes restaurant; a terrine of wild rabbit, a mosaic of fish and the sommelier's recommended Chateaux Saint-Baillon rosé 1995. It was very tempting to go all the way and have the 1893 Percenade Armagnac at £29 a glass. No, that will be the celebration when Scotland beat Morocco.

Tuesday, 23 June

It is Saint-Etienne's day of the saltire. The Scots have taken over the steps of the town hall and designated it a terracing. A group of fans have invaded the balcony to display a massive saltire with a caricature of Jacques Chirac playing the bagpipes. The legend reads: 'Jacques Chirac is a Scotsman'. Even the council bin lorry in the main square is flying Scotland's emblem.

Susan Spalding, a student from Edinburgh, is painting saltires on the fingernails of Scottish female fans. She and her friends are also bravely painting Braveheart-style motifs on various parts of the anatomy of male supporters.

The whole town is *en fête*. Gary, Craig and the other Gary from Glasgow continue to meet exceptional hospitality. They went into the bank to exchange some cash. The manager came out from his office and asked them to sit down at a table in the reception area. Minutes later he appeared with a delegation of his female staff and champagne and proceded to pour out celebratory glasses for all.

• The Scots are at their usual trick of forming a roadblock so that cars have to stop, handshakes are compulsory and women are kissed. It is at this point that I meet the only truly nasty Scots fan of the entire campaign. Our man's contribution was not to shake hands with them but to blow cigarette smoke in their faces. When a French lady of Arabic extraction complained, someone in this chap's group spat on the windscreen.

In subsequent conversation, he reveals that he is a chartered accountant and speaks of his hopes of imminent advancement in that profession. With the qualities he showed here he obviously has a golden future liquidating, sequestrating and generally blowing smoke in the face of society.

• The time for the match approaches. Inevitably, M. le Maire has abandoned his plan to give a literary talk in the bar of Le Glasgow, in which the fans are hanging from the rafters. It is also the time for the walk to the stadium. Behind the massed pipers, the Tartan Army marches into folklore along the main street. It is an occasion which will never be forgotten by Scots or French alike.

It is awesome. The kilted ones, 20 abreast, striding as if towards some battle. (Little did they know it was to be a Culloden.) But thankfully there are the lunatics to provide the comic relief. There is a chap on top of the bus shelter urging the fans to louder and more raucous singing and using a litre bottle of Irn Bru as his conductor's baton. There is a kiltie who has climbed 100 feet up a crane to hang his saltire.

• The match in the Geoffroy-Guichard stadium was not the Scotland's team finest hour. We are defining our tragedy again. This time it is underlined three times, once for each Moroccan goal. There is palpable pain in the Scottish support. One Scottish fan throws away his fur coat in disgust. Yes, his fur coat. He came to the match in fur coat and kilt and nothing else. I would ask him to explain the outfit but somehow there seems no point.

• Thankfully the game is over. Scotland are out in the first round yet again. Bizarrely, so are the Moroccans because Norway drew with Brazil. As we all troop out of the stadium, Gregg from Glasgow says: 'It could have been worse. We could have won and still not qualified.' There seems to be no end to the ways Scotland can define tragedy.

Outside the stadium, the Wee-ist Pipe Band in the World, are putting our World Cup campaign decently to rest. Fans gather silently in a circle, some of them weeping, as piper Kevin plays 'The Flooers o' the Forest'. The band finish their lament, pause for a respectable moment, then lead the retreat from the stadium playing 'Scotland the Brave'.

But we are not brave. We are subdued. The atmosphere is as flat as the team's performance. We take consolation in shaking hands with the Moroccan fans and the French police. The hand-shaking is about the only work the French polis have had to do all night.

• An hour after the game the Scots are back frolicking in the fountains of Saint-Etienne, but many are running empty – as empty as their wallets after a fortnight in France. Others are more positive. They are singing: 'We're the famous Tartan Army and we're off to Tokyo.' This is a reference to the World Cup 2002 in Japan and South Korea. Some of the mad bastards mean it.

• When all else fails, the Tartan Army takes refuge and delight in expressing in many and varied forms how much they hate the English. Most of us enjoy an English reversal, but there has to be more to life. Cammy, from Fife, is a true Scottish fan. The look of grief on his face when Morocco scored their third goal said more than any words. Two nights before in Le Glasgow pub, as the fans launched for perhaps the hundredth time into the song about standing up or sitting down if you hate the English, Cammy stood on a table and suggested vociferously that we sing about Scotland.

• The Saint-Etienne people have taken kindly to the Scottish way of celebrating. Even a tough and serious-looking French police sergeant was persuaded to pose for a photograph clutching a Tweety Pie stuffed toy in a tartan outfit. The Tartan Army will never be short of recruits. A young man wearing a Scotland top stops and sways at our table in a café in the square. He is quite drunk. He is eating a chip baguette and is clutching a can of beer. He is slurring the words 'Irn Bru, Irn Bru, Irn Bru . . .' When he finally manages to speak we realise he is French.

• For you Tommy, the World Cup is over. I am walking across the town hall square in Saint-Etienne. A voice calls out: 'Mr Shields! Mr Shields!' Two young fans are preparing to sleep in the square, using their saltire as a blanket and the plinth of a statue as a pillow. 'Mr Shields, can you tuck us in and tell us a bedtime story.' Once upon a time there was a Scotland football team who qualified for the second stage of the World Cup . . .

Going Home

Any analysis of France '98 has to include the cost. It has been galling to watch the profiteering as hotel prices were openly hiked by 50 per cent or more. Bars cynically took advantage of fans who were either not able to work out the going rate for a beer or didn't care. Ticket touting was rampant among the French, from the highest official to the lowest.

Michel Platini himself recognised this when asked in an interview about the ticket-scalping. There will always be 'pigeons' prepared to pay the price, he said. At France '98, the pigeons were well and truly plucked.

• Some Scotland can't get home quickly enough once the dream is over. We hear of one fan who is going home a different person. So keen is he for a sharp exit that he has swapped air tickets and passports with a friend who is taking a longer route home. It seems unlikely. Another of these Tartan Army myths.

I am going home as fast as I can but it necessitates two overnight stays in France. In the gardens of a château near Maçon which takes in paying guests, I get a chance to ponder on the whole experience. I decide not even to attempt to rationalise the last three weeks in terms of sport, politics, or culture. I decide just to enjoy the plate of frogs' legs and the bottle of Chassagne-Montrachet.

If how we follow football defines a nation, then Scotland would appear to be a country of amiable drunks in kilts and Jimmy hats. But we are more than that. I feel as if I should examine who the Scots are and where we are going as a nation. But thre are other, more pressing questions. Should I have the Sauternes or the St Croix du Mont with the pudding?

• The second stop on the retreat from France '98 is in the northern town of Arras. It is an opportunity to find the grave of my grandfather John Shields who was killed on the Somme in 1916. But any plans to linger in this poignantly beautiful part of France have to be abandoned.

England are playing a match at Lens, which is only ten miles away, and the entire region is under siege and curfew because of the English hooligans. *Les bêtes anglais* are despoiling the very piece of ground their great-grandfathers fought to free in the First World War and under which soil many of these ancestors are buried.

I board the ferry at Calais and leave France '98 proud to be Scottish with a firmer sense of who we are and where we are going and with a much firmer knowledge of who we are not.

Postscript

Following Scotland is an affliction and an addiction. I had meant to take a sabbatical after France '98 and, under no circumstances, subject myself to the qualifying rounds of the Euro 2000 championship which began in September, barely ten weeks after our defeat in Saint-Etienne.

Against my better judgement, I found myself in Vilnius amidst 500 hardcore Tartan Army supporting Scotland and Lithuania.

Day One

In the course of following the Scottish football team I have been led astray by many people. The list includes plumbers, policemen, film producers, and university professors. Here I am in Lithuania and for the first time I have been led astray by lawyers.

I should have been in the office writing about important matters such as the Scottish parliament and the strength or weakness of the rouble. Then Bishop & Robertson Chalmers, solicitors of Glasgow and Edinburgh, insisted that I join them for a trip to their Vilnius office to see at first hand the economic and commercial links being forged between Lithuania and Scotland.

The trip happens to coincide with tomorrow's Euro 2000 qualifying match here between the two countries. It sounds like fun but have you ever tried singing 'We're on the march with Bishop & Robertson Chalmers'?

• According to one of my local guides, the Lithuanians don't understand the Scots. Not just the language barrier or the slightly eccentric behaviour of the small number of the Tartan Army who have gathered here. The Lithuanians cannot understand why Scotland is not an independent country.

Scotland is an identifiable nation with a big-enough population and a reasonable economy, so why is it not governing its own affairs. If Lithuania can do it with a population of 3.7million, a long history of being occupied by Russians, Poles and Germans then why can't Scotland?

• As part of re-inventing their nation after throwing off the Soviet yoke, the Lithuanians got rid of an awful lot of statues of Lenin and Karl Marx. But there is a new statue which is a must-see on any tour of old Vilnius town. It is a bronze bust of Frank Zappa, the rock legend who died in 1993. As far as we can ascertain there is no conection between Mr Zappa and Lithuania. But the Lithuanian Frank Zappa appreciation society thought the statue was a good idea. They appear to be very much in the minority.

But a visit to the Zappa is more cheerful than a couple of the other attractions on the tourist trail – the former KGB headquarters where the cells still have blood on the walls and a forest clearing outside of town called the Killing Fields complete with skulls and bones where the KGB also practised their black arts. Or you can visit the TV tower in Vilnius to see the bullet holes left by the Soviet troops from their failed attempt to suppress the independence movement in 1991.

• The Tartan Army have taken quite kindly to Vilnius. The fact that it is populated by extremely statuesque blonde and red-headed ladies may have something to do with it.

Other inducements include the local strong lager at about £1 a pint. Pubs stay open until 6 a.m.

The language is rather complicated and it is unlikely that most of the Tartan visitors will get much beyond *du alus* (two beers) and *aciu* (thank you). *Aciu* is easy to remember. It is pronounced atchoo.

• There is plenty of cheap and filling food to be had. But only the brave are attempting the cepelinai. These are huge potato dumplings stuffed with meat. Just how huge can be guessed from the fact that name cepelinai comes from Zeppelin, the German chap of airship fame.

Your average Scot might manage one of these cepelinai, if they are not put off by the sea of congealing grease in which they are served. The Lithuanians would regard this as something of a wimpish quantity and claim they can consume a dozen at a sitting.

As part of their becoming a nation once again, the Lithuanian Language Commission has been excising foreign-based words from their language. They tried to do so with cepelinai declaring it illegal because of its German origin. Their suggested alternative was didzkukuliai. It has not caught on.

• A restaurant called Ritos Smukle is the place for those who wish to confront Lithuanian home cooking head on. As well as the lead zeppelins, black bread is much in evidence. Stuffed with garlic and deep-fried it makes an interesting nibble with your beer; as riga, a sweet fermented drink made from black bread, it is less appealing.

• Scottish football fans on a tight budget are used to sleeping in railway stations. In Vilnius they can do so in sightly more comfort than they are used to. For £2.50 you can book a bed in a railway carriage. It is advisable not to sleep in after the 8 a.m. alarm call if you don't want to go on an unscheduled journey.

• Vilnius has avoided much of the gangsterism which afflicts other parts of the former Soviet Union but there are still a few hard cases around town. They are skinhead Nazis who are not in the business of accepting the hand of friendship.

The British Embassy has issued a list of pubs and clubs which should be given a wide berth. As if the local drink is not strong enough, some of the less than friendly denizens have a habit of adding a sleeping draught to a visitor's drink to facilitate the subsequent mugging.

The skinheads who lie in wait outside certain of these premises seeking to inflict some random pain on passing tourists. They are even more dangerous than the cepelinai potato dumplings.

• Some of the Scots are fraternising with the ladies of the night who haunt the larger hotels. This gives rise to one overheard conversation.

FIRST SCOT: 'I was in bed wi' wan o' thae Russian hoors. She was keen to get oan wi' the shagging but ah wantit tae watch the Danny Kaye movie oan the telly.'

SECOND SCOT: 'Which wan?'

FIRST SCOT: 'Natasha.'

SECOND SCOT: 'Naw, which movie?'

Day Two

The main problem for Scotland fans over here in Lithuania is that the country does not appear to have a species of animal under threat. In the Faroes we sang 'We're the famous Tartan Army and we're here to save the whale.' In France this became 'we're here to save the snail'.

They eat a variety of strange foods in Lithuania but none seem to fit the bill. As part of the immersion in local colour, your correspondent had for his tea a portion of smoked sturgeon to start followed by 'a collection of wild meats'. The wild meats turned out to be venison and wild boar and very nice too. But not the stuff of musical lyrics, I fear.

• In the search for rhyme, Lithuania is a bit of a dead loss. But the capital, Vilnius fits the bill nicely. To the tune of 'holi-holiday' the fans have come up with the pithy couplet: 'We're in Vilnius and we're on the piss . . .'

• I mentioned in an earlier dispatch that with the fall of the Soviet empire, the statues of Lenin and other heroes of the revolution have been turn down and, for no apparent reason, a bust has been erected of singer Frank Zappa. This has caused some debate about which famous Lithuanian should be commemorated in statue form. The answer is Billy McNeill of Celtic.

Billy's grandparents were Lithuanian, part of the great migration from these parts to darkest North Lanarkshire. An explanation may be necessary, including why he is called Caesar. Another candidate could be Jock Stein, another North Lanarkshire man rumoured to have a bit of Lithuanian in him.

•There is a trio of Tartan Army chaps from Fife whose philosophy is to spend as little as possible on accommodation. They are bunked three to a double room with one of them in a sleeping bag. He told the hotel receptionist he has to sleep on the floor because of his bad back. This means they are paying £5 each per night. This includes a coupon for breakfast. They tend to rise too late for this meal but have negotiated that each coupon can be used for a 200ml bottle of vodka for their own version of breakfast.

• The Tartan Army got a less than than warm welcome from the British Airways cabin crew who drew the short straw to bring out the advance party on Wednesday. Okay, some of the fans were a touch naughty. One of them was drinking and smoking as he walked across the tarmac. Another drink-impaired individual was judged only just fit to fly but unfit to walk and was oxtered aboard.

Apart from this, it was a normal Tartan Army flight, possibly a bit quieter than most. But diplomacy was not on the agenda as the cabin staff made it very clear the Scottish fans were not welcome. They even went as far as saying in the announcement before landing that they wished 'to thank the cabin staff for putting up with what has been a very bad flight'.

Stung by this insult, the fans responded with a song for the stewardess who appeared to be in a particularly bad mood. They sang: 'She's grumpy, grumpy, very very grumpy. She's very grumpy' followed by 'Grumpy, grumpy, give us a wave'. Which Mrs Grumpy duly did and the flight ended on a happier note.

Day Three

I am sorry to lapse into bad language but the kilted one exiting miserably from the stadium in Vilnius after the miserabe 0-0 draw had it right when he sang: 'We're shite but the vodka's cheap.' Once again the Tartan Army had to take solace in strong drink and the fact that while our tired old team had drawn the English had lost.

An increasing number of English voices are to be heard among the Scottish support with the bizarre scene in Vilnius old town of a chap in a Scotland top singing in a London accent: 'My old man said be an England fan. I told him not be a silly person.' The last word may not necessarily have been 'person' but we're trying to keep it clean here.

• The major consolation for any member of the Scotland Travel Club is to meet the lovely Marjory Nimmo. Marjory works tirelessly and cheerfully to look after the fans and in return she is garlanded with flowers, offers of marriage and general adoration. Outside the Valgris Stadium before the match the Adoration of the Marjory was done in fish. The fish, like oversized goldfish, were part of the catering on offer. No Scots fan could contemplate eating one but a Stonehavenite thought it was an ideal present for Marjory.

As she stood holding her fish, there was speculation that with a bread roll from the hot dog stand, the blessed Marjory could feed the entire Tartan Army at half-time. Or even better work a miracle with the team.

• It will not surprise you to hear that the Tartan Army members can get confused. One fan in the bar of the Hotel Leituva was singing the Marseillaise and engaging locals with 'Comment allez-vous?' A friend was on hand to explain: 'Jimmy, we're in Lithuania.' The fans still have fond memories of France '98, particularly Bordeaux, and there are various plans afoot for a return. One supporter even has fond memories of the French prices. Gazing at his immense handful of litas notes, the Lithuanian currency which comes in at six to the pound and in some bars at three to the pint, he said: 'Try as I might, I just cannae seem to get rid o' this stuff.'

• It is well-known that when even the smallest, most rotund and hacket-featured Scotsman dons a kilt he becomes irresistible to even supermodel women. The locals have expressed admiration for the persistence of the Scots in the face of the truth that the above theory is not always the case.

A Baltic person, Thomas from Tallinn, who was at the game with Scottish friends, was surprised to see so many of the Tartan Army had brought with them their wives, girlfriends or bideys-in. 'Why are they bringing wolves to the forest?' he asked, which is a Baltic way of talking about coals to Newcastle.

• A member of the Dutch Tartan Army ran into a spot of bother bringing his wolf to the forest. The Scot, who works in a car factory in Holland, travelled to Vilnius by train with his Dutch bidey-in. They were whiling away the hours as they traversed Poland with a spot of R&R. The railway guard burst in and informed them that their conjugal activity was illegal on trains in Poland, even in the privacy of their own sleeping compartment.

At the next stop, the guard summoned both the police and the army. The Dutch girl realised that the whole thing was a ploy to extract money from them. She told the guard, the police and the army that there was no cash forthcoming and she would take it to the highest authorities. They retreated unpaid.

•Another culinary note. The item 'hedgehog with crackling'

proved too tempting for a group of fans. They all ordered the hedgehog supper. Most of them could not eat the stodgy, rubbery, white meat which came wrapped in doughballs. One chap, obviously with an iron constitution, manged to eat all of his. 'You realise, Sammy,' said his pal, 'that your next shite is gonny be a hedegehog.' Which brings us back to the Scotland team's performance.

• An intriguing overheard comment: 'But he managed to swim to safety . . .' This transpires to be the conclusion to the tale of a Tartan Army regular who was foolish enough to accept a lift from four Lithuanian bruisers. Instead of taking him to his hotel they drove him to a forest where they stole his money and proceeded to beat him up. He managed to escape. They gave chase but gave up when he plunged into a river and swam to the other side. Asked later how he felt about this experience, our veteran kilted one replied: 'These things happen.'

It was then that I realised that I am not cut out to be a genuine Tartan Army member, braving the rigours of Eastern Europe and other hard places. Take me back to Bordeaux.